IMPLEMENTATION OF PROBLEM-BASED LEARNING IN HIGHER EDUCATION

Implementation of Problem-based Learning
in Higher Education

Edited by

Erik de Graaff & Peter A.J. Bouhuijs

THESIS PUBLISHERS
AMSTERDAM 1993

CIP-DATA KONINKLIJKE BIBLIOTHEEK, DEN HAAG

Implementation

Implementation of problem-based learning in higher
education / Erik de Graaff & Peter A.J. Bouhuijs (eds.).-
Amsterdam: Thesis Publishers
With ref.
ISBN 90-5170-209-4
NUGI 742
Subject headings: problem-based learning ; higher
education / higher education ; innovation.

Coverdesign Mirjam Bode

ISBN 90-5170-209-4
NUGI 742

Contents

List of contributors

Charles Anderson, Phd.   University of Edinburgh, Edinburgh

Peter A. J. Bouhuijs, Phd.   University of Limburg, Maastricht

Herman van den Bosch, Phd.   University of Nijmegen, Nijmegen

Marcel P.J.G. Claessens, MA. Delft University of Technology, Delft

Th. Olle ten Cate, Phd.   University of Amsterdam, Amsterdam

Jan van Driel, Phd.   Delft University of Technology, Delft

Pieter H.A.M. Frijns, Phd.   Delft University of Technology, Delft

Wim H. Gijselaers, Phd.   University of Limburg, Maastricht

Erik de Graaff, Phd.   Delft University of Technology, Delft

Wim M.G. Jochems, Phd.   Delft University of Technology, Delft

Egbert Schadé Phd.   University of Amsterdam, Amsterdam

Kees van Wijngaarden, MA. Delft University of Technology, Delft

Jos Willems, Phd.   University of Nijmegen, IOWO, Nijmegen

Outline of the book

This book deals with the implementation of problem-based learning in higher education in the Netherlands. The chapters in the book are based on papers presented at a symposium on the implementation of problem-based learning at the ECER-conference at Enschede 22-25 june 1992, with the addition of a few related papers form the theme higher education.

The book opens with an introduction on the principles of problem-based learning by De Graaff. Next, aspects of the implementation of PBL are presented in three sections.

The first section of the book focusses on the organizational aspects of the implementation of PBL. Bouhuijs and De Graaff describe the introduction of PBL at the Faculty of Building Sciences in Delft, and De Graaff and Bouhuijs elaborate on the organizational principles of curriculum change. An extraordinary solution for the problems of managing a PBL-curriculum is the concept of the "school", discussed by Van den Bosch and Gijselaers in chapter 4, in relation to the introduction of PBL at the Faculty of Policy and Administrative Sciences in Nijmegen.

The second section consists of three chapters deals with consequences of the conversion to a PBL-curriculum, with the Faculty of Building Sciences in Delft serving as an example. The importance of faculty development in the conversion to PBL is stressed by Van Driel in chapter 5. In chapter 6 Claessens and Jochems describe the development of a systematic approach to program-evaluation and the consequences with respect student assessment methods are analyzed in chapter 7, by Frijns and De Graaff.

The third section contains four studies on the effects of PBL. The relationship of group size with instructional techniques is analyzed by Jochems, in chapter 8. Chapter 9, by Van Wijngaarden en Willems describes a study on the "directing effects" of study tasks. Students perception of tutorial groups, in the traditional sense is investigated in chapter 10, by Anderson and the combination of PBL with traditional methods in medical education is investigated by Ten Cate and Schadé in chapter 11.

We hope this book provides useful information for those who consider the introduction of PBL, or who are already in the process of converting their educational program.

Erik de Graaff
Peter Bouhuijs

chapter 1

Introduction: the principles of problem based learning

Erik de Graaff

Introduction

Teaching and learning are often considered to be complementary. The teacher pours out knowledge that is absorbed by the students. In its very nature, however, learning is an active process, involving the intentional focusing of attention and subsequent digestion of information. It could very well be possible that the often encountered discrepancies between actual learning results and the learning goals stipulated by the teacher are caused by the fact that students simply loose their interest in learning. Students are mature human beings with a mind of their own. And, the study behavior of adults is more effective when they see the reason for what they are doing (Knowles, 1969). Problem-based learning (PBL) provides such "reasons for learning" by presenting students with practice related problem-tasks. Consequently, PBL-students are expected to define their own learning goals and to pursue actively the accumulation of knowledge and skills.

Over the past decades PBL has spread around the world. It is considered "the most important innovation in education for the professions for many years" (Boud and Feletti, 1991, p.13). Yet, the same authors denounce PBL to be controversial, and the introduction of PBL in an existing institution is considered a hazardous enterprise (Schmidt, 1991). The debate on PBL is often obscured by different views on the question: what are the essential elements of this method? The addition of yet another definition of PBL does not solve the problem. Rather than trying to determine what does and what does not meet the specifications of "real" PBL, I would prefer to explore the possibilities that PBL offers to higher education, with an open mind to adaptation and experimentation. For better understanding, however, it may be useful to know the main characteristics of the PBL-approach and to be aware of the background of the development of this method. In the following sections the roots of PBL will be as it has become known in the Netherlands will be surveyed.

The origin of problem-based learning

Problem-based learning, as we know it today, was first developed at the medical school of McMaster University in Canada (Spaulding, 1969; Neufeld & Barrows, 1974; Fraenkel, 1978; Barrows & Tamblyn, 1980). Criticism on the conventional medical education was an important motivator for the designers of a completely new innovative curriculum. Medical science had evolved into a finely branched network of highly specialized fields. The traditional curricula reflected this trend of specialization. In the first years the groundwork of "basic disciplines" was laid. In later years students were confronted with separate courses in the major specialties. The relationship between disciplines and specialties and with actual medical practice, was left for the students, to find out for them selves after graduation.

By contrast the problem-based approach focuses on the integration of knowledge and skills from different domains. Application in practice is deemed more important than storing facts by rote learning. In the context of medical education this implies that learning centers on the patient and his complaint. By systematically analyzing such patient problems, students formulate questions with respect to the information they lack to solve a problem and so select their own learning-goals. Right from the start students learn to integrate knowledge from different disciplines, related to the same medical problem. At the same time they acquaint themselves with the problem-solving process of a physician. This way the relevance of the material studied is assured, but also the experience of learning is more exciting and more meaningful. Trained as independent learners, PBL-students may be expected to be able to identify and fill gaps in their knowledge, also after graduation. Typically, in PBL, the learning process is stimulated by means of small group work (Barrows, 1986). This provides students the opportunity to learn to work together like the members of a small medical team.

The features discussed so far, are not unique to PBL. There is a long history of case-based learning and the method of project education has an even closer relationship to actual practice than PBL (Van Woerden, 1991). The process of self-directed learning in the tutorial groups leans on the concepts of learning by experience as advocated by Jerôme Bruner (Schmidt, 1983) and the ideas of Carl Rogers on student centered learning (Rogers, 1961). In a sense it could be said that the definition of the role of the tutor is as old as Socrates, who compared his role as a teacher to that of a midwife easing the birth of knowledge. Therefore, we may conclude that the innovative aspect of PBL can be located in the combination of educational techniques aimed at the cultivation of independent learning behavior and the consequent exploitation of the relationship with actual practice.

The Maastricht version of PBL

In the Netherlands PBL was introduced at the Medical Faculty of the Limburg State University. The founders of this new medical school shared with the founding fathers of McMaster the view that medical education needs to be flexible in order to be able to adapt to changing needs of society (Basisfilosofie, 1972). There are continuously epidemiological and demographic shifts in the population and as a result of the rapid technological developments in biomedical science knowledge rapidly becomes obsolete. Consequently, medical education should place less emphasis on factual knowledge: "the professional education of physicians should emphasize the acquisition and development of skills values and attitudes by students at least to the same extent that they do their acquisition of knowledge" (Walton, 1985, p.1).

The Maastricht medical school was among the first to adapt the principles of problem-based learning. In the Netherlands PBL has become known chiefly in the Maastricht version. Characteristics of the PBL curriculum are (Moust, Schmidt, & Bouhuijs, 1989):

* integration of disciplines and skills
* curriculum structure with thematic blocks
* learning oriented work in small groups
* self-directed learning

One of the main features of the PBL-curriculum is the thematic organization that replaces the traditional array of disciplines and majors. The four-year preclinical phase of the Maastricht medical curriculum consists out of six-week thematic blocks. Small multidisciplinary teams of faculty members are responsible for the content of the "block books". The theme is introduced to the students by means of study tasks (problems, descriptions of patient cases or other phenomena related to the current theme). Typically, students analyze the problems in groups of 8-10 students, that meet on a regular basis (Schmidt & Bouhuijs, 1980; Moust et. al, 1989). The tutor, the staff-member that supervises the sessions is not necessarily an expert with respect to the issues at hand. Consequently, the tutor is not the one that provides the answers. Students are expected to elaborate on their prior knowledge in order to come to understand the problem. In the course of this process they find out where they lack important information, resulting in the formulation of learning goals. The acquired insights are discussed in the next session. In addition to the small group-work, skills training and practice orientation are scheduled. A large proportion of study time is reserved for independent self-study.

Application in other fields

At first PBL has been implemented mainly within the context of health education (medicine, nursing, fysiotherapy). Gradually these educational methods are also being applied in programmes for other professions like law, economics, business administration, architecture, mechanical engineering, industrial design. However, since each profession has its own traditions and characteristics, the principles of problem-based learning need to be adapted to suit the specific demands of each situation. As a consequence several varieties of problem-based learning have emerged and the ongoing expansion will lead to even more diversity.

The implementation of PBL in an existing institution raises questions like:
* Can we just pick some aspects that we like without altering the over-all structure of our school?
* Which characteristics will adapt easily to our conditions?
* What organizational problems will arise in the process of implementation?

Just like it was done in McMaster and in Maastricht, in each case one must ask the question: what kind of professionals do we like to educate? If you need highly specialized technical experts, there is no rationale for a thematic structure of the curriculum. If the profession is based on a substantial body of unchanging knowledge the professionals must master absolutely, you miss the grounds for self-directed learning. When you are training professionals that chiefly operate solitary, the tutorial groups loose their point of exercising team work. In general it can be said that PBL works for professions with a multidisciplinary background and a non-specialized interdisciplinary practice. Evidently, professions will vary in the degree to which these criteria are met.

The basic principles of PBL, that learning should be oriented towards practice right from the start and that students should be activated, can be operationalized by an array of means. Adaptation of the principles of PBL involves the argumentation which elements are kept and which elements are left out. For instance, lectures and directive study assignments that were banned in the original PBL, can be integrated with problem-tasks, on the grounds that students do not have enough prior knowledge to discuss the complex subject unaided (De Graaff & Merx, 1984). Within the framework of PBL new elements can be creatively added. Instead of the written casehistory to be discussed in the tutorial group, study activities could be stimulated just as well by visual presentations, simulation of practice, role playing, or the dissection of an extended casehistory by an expert. In any case the test of the educational method is the extend to which it is effective in reaching its purpose: to provide students with operational knowledge and skills for professional practice.

References

Barrows, H.S. (1986) A taxonomy of problem-based learning methods. **Medical Education,** 20, 481-486.

Barrows, H.S. & Tamblyn, R.M. (1980) **Problem-Based Learning: An Approach to Medical Education,** New York: Springer.

Basisfilosofie (basic philosophy) (1972) Maastricht: Rijksuniversiteit Limburg.
Boud, D. (ed.) (1985) **Problem-based-learning in education for the professions.** Sydney: Higher Education Research and Development Society of Australia.

Boud, D. & Feletti, G. (1991) **The Challenge of Problem-based Learning.** London: Kogan Page.

Fraenkel, G.J. (1978) McMaster Revisited. **British Medical Journal,** 2, 1072-1076.

De Graaff, E & R. Merx (1984) **Variatie in onderwijsvormen binnen probleemgestuurd onderwijs.** (Variations in educational format within the context of PBL). Eindhoven: University of Technology.

Knowles, M.S. (1969) **The modern practice of adult education.** New York: Association Press.

Moust, J.C.H., Bouhuijs, P.A.J. & Schmidt, H.G. (1989). **Probleemgestuurd leren.** [Problem-based Learning]. Groningen: Wolters-Noordhoff.

Neufeld, V. & Barrows, H.S. (1974). The Mc Master Philosophy: An approach to medical education. **Journal of Medical Education,** 49, 1040-1050.

Rogers, C. (1961) **On becoming a person.** Boston: Houghton Mifflin.

Schmidt, H.J. (1983) Problem-based learning: rationale and description. **Medical Education,** 17, 11-16.

Schmidt, H.J. (1991) Onderwijskundige aspekten van probleemgestuurd onderwijs. In W.S. Jochems (red.), **Activerend Onderwijs, over onderwijsvormen die het leren bevorderen** [Activating Education, on educational formats that encourage learning]. Delft: Delft Universitaire pers.

Schmidt, H.J. & Bouhuijs, P.A.J. (1980) **Onderwijs in taakgerichte groepen.** (Task-directed groups educational groups). Utrecht: Het Spektrum.

Spaulding, W.P. (1969) The Undergraduate Medical Curriculum Model: McMaster University. **Canadian Medical Association Journal,** 100, 659-664.

Walton, H.J. (1985) Primary healthcare in European medical education: a survey. **Medical Education,** 19, 167-188.

Van Woerden, W.M. (1991) **Het Projectonderwijs onderzocht.** (Research into the project method of teaching). thesis, Enschede: University of Technology Twente.

Part I

Organizational Aspects of the Implementation of PBL

The introduction of a problem-based curriculum at the Faculty of Building Sciences

Peter A.J. Bouhuijs & Erik de Graaff

Introduction

Innovation of a university curriculum is an operation affecting many people. The literature on educational innovation suggests careful procedures of planning, development and implementation in order to involve the participants (Dalin, 1978; Saylor et al, 1981; Fullan, 1982; Romiszowski, 1984). According to this view the success of an educational innovation depends upon the degree to which it is adopted by the participants and therefore on the degree to which it is perceived by them as instrumental to reach their personal and professional goals. Under stable external conditions, large scale educational changes are scarce and usually take a long time. The introduction of problem-based learning in existing programmes is no exception to that rule. In medical education problem-based learning is still considered a method which can only be applied in new schools. Although several schools have disproved this belief now for some years by shifting to PBL completely (i.e. the medical schools of Sherbrooke and Bowman Gray) or by starting parallel PBL programmes to their existing curriculum (i.e. the medical schools of New Mexico and Michigan State University), a complete change to PBL in existing schools is still rare.
A long development process to involve participants in an organization before actually implementing a new curriculum is sound advice when the organization can make its own decisions. In this chapter we describe a school, which decided under severe external pressure to change its curriculum, and to introduce problem-based learning. In this case the ideal approach to innovation could not be followed. Is it possible to introduce a complex curricular change under external pressure and will it be accepted by faculty and students? In this chapter we will describe the initial part of the change process which took place at the Faculty of Building Sciences of Delft University of Technology in 1989 and 1990.

The problems

Like in most European countries the eighties were difficult times for Dutch higher education institutions. In The Netherlands the economic situation forced the government to change its long-term policy of expansion of higher education. New budget systems were introduced for undergraduate education resulting in a lower appropriation; the duration of master degree programmes was reduced; research grants were no longer dependent upon student numbers, but awarded on a competitive basis; faculties were forced to cooperate or merge with other programmes; the number of senior staff positions was reduced, and a general salary cut for teaching staff was introduced. As a result of these and other measures, public expenditure on higher education dropped between 1983 and 1987. The Faculty of Building Sciences, a large school with about 2000 students, was hit hard by these policy changes. Like most faculties in Universities of Technology the Faculty of Building Sciences had opposed the policies and as a reaction refused to introduce real changes. The curriculum was compressed rather than reduced, resulting in abundance and unbalance. Substantial study delays manifested themselves. Virtually no one was able to complete the curriculum within the nominal duration of four years and only 22% of the students graduated within the maximum allotted time of six years (Statistisch jaarboek '88/'89). Within the University of Technology the Faculty of Building Sciences had a special position because of its "arts" character. In the sixties the faculty developed a curriculum according to the principles of project education. Architectural design, practice orientation and integration of knowledge stood at the core of this program. Basically the curriculum consisted of a series of design projects sustained by discipline oriented courses and skills exercises. Students could choose from over 1000 different courses and projects. The system of project education had gradually deteriorated. There were large differences in quality of different projects, integration with other parts of the curriculum often failed and the programmes were almost impossible to manage, and finally the costs were too high.

Early 1989 the problems of Building Sciences became acute. The university board imposed a cut on the faculty budget of about ten percent. Due to earlier cuts the flexibility to accommodate again without questioning its policies proved fairly limited for the faculty. An even more serious threat followed soon. A national external review committee published a report on the various Dutch programmes for architecture and building sciences in polytechnics and universities of technology. The report was highly critical about the Delft faculty of Building Sciences. The main criticism on the educational programme included:

* the graduate profile is too much focused on design careers
* a weak input of science and technology in the courses
* little cohesion in the curriculum
* unclear organizational structures

The review committee advised the government to concentrate building sciences in one, rather than two faculties. Based on this report the minister of education and science suggested that the faculty of building sciences in Delft should merge with another building school, or with another faculty in Delft, or simply close down. The report and the reaction of the government got wide publicity. Newspapers published several articles about the problems of Building Sciences in Delft. Faced with this serious threat of annihilation the faculty board decided to fight for survival and to change the faculty drastically. Three main points were stressed:

* a change in organizational and financial management
* the redirection of research programmes
* a paradigm shift in education

In this chapter we will confine ourselves to the educational side of the reorganization. One year before the report of the External Review Committee the faculty board already had started internal reviews, which resulted in recommendations to introduce changes in the curriculum. When the external review report arrived, it was therefore relatively easy to introduce the Program Committee Building Sciences (PKB) with the task to generate a proposal for a new curriculum within six months. This committee chaired by the associate dean for educational affairs consisted of key teachers and student representatives. In line with the major criticisms of the external review the committee was asked to address a change in

18

the content profile of the curriculum, as well to look for more efficient and effective teaching methods. Since it was vital for the survival to show quickly major changes, external consultants were hired to help the faculty to draft plans in these areas. The first author was appointed as an educational consultant at that time. The faculty board deliberately used the external pressure and the limited time available to force the school into major change. After three afternoon meetings the committee decided to organize a three day retreat to draft an outline plan which could be further developed during the summer. A small team of external consultants planned the agenda and chaired the meetings. The major aim of the conference was to get commitment of key persons in the faculty for a radical change. During this conference PBL was introduced as a strategy to cope with some of the major problems in the school. Conference participants worked in small groups to discuss how PBL could be used in the faculty, to develop a first outline of a thematic line for the first year programme, and to discuss the general structure of a new curriculum. The retreat was a strategic success. The development of a new programme was not longer considered a necessary burden, but as a challenge to revitalize the ideals of the school. As one of the key persons described it: "to me, this conference was the best event in the school since the student revolution of 1968."

Why PBL?

Problem-based learning (PBL) appeared to be a way to tackle several problems at the same time. The choice for a new instructional strategy showed the outside critics that a substantial change was set in motion. Yet at the same time PBL seemed to fit in nicely with the educational tradition of apprenticeship to a practitioner (Maitland, 1991). Inside the school PBL could be considered as a structured way of project work, the major instructional approach used in the existing programme. PBL could provide a curricular structure, in which important, but unfulfilled goals of project work could be reached. In particular the stronger organizational framework and the integration of various disciplines seemed to get a better chance in a PBL approach (Bouhuijs, 1990). It was also considered a good way to tackle the inefficiencies in student progress in the curriculum. Studies of the problem-based Maastricht medical curriculum compared to other Dutch medical schools (Post et al, 1988) indicated a lower attrition rate and a shorter time to graduate in a PBL curriculum. The Maastricht model of PBL also includes other aspects which proved to be highly attractive to overcome some of the other problems in Delft. In particular the centralized control over the curriculum, quality control by systematic programme evaluation (Gijselaers, 1990), and the assessment system (Van der Vleuten & Verwijnen, 1990) were considered as attractive features. The emphasis on structured training of medical skills (Bouhuijs et al.,1987; Van Dalen, 1990) triggered a discussion about the feasibility of a more structured way to teach designing.

The draft plan

In September 1989 a draft report was produced which was used inside and outside the faculty. The report contained an analysis of the problems, an outline of a new curriculum, and introduced PBL as an instructional strategy for the new programme. It also contained proposals for new organizational structures for planning and monitoring the new curriculum. Instead of a defensive report opposing outside criticisms, the report presented a fresh view for the future. Special information meetings were organized for staff en students to explain the proposals and to introduce the concept of problem-based learning. Due to other measures, such as lay-offs, the general climate was rather negative with regard to the faculty board and their external consultants. The faculty council reacted highly critical. Many council members still didn't want to support a major change and complained about the lack of continuity between the existing programme and the proposed new curriculum. Since key teachers defended the committee report however, the faculty council postponed its judgement till they had received the final report. Outside the school the draft report was used for consultation purposes with other faculties, the university board, professional organizations, and government officials. The external reactions were generally supportive and contained feedback which could be used for the further development of the plans. The consultations also had a clear public relations effect. The faculty presented itself as an organization ready to take the challenge to make real changes. Since a major point in the criticism had been the disbelief that Building Sciences could change its course, the mere existence of a report announcing major changes was an important signal.

The final report

In October 1989 the Committee organized a second working conference of two days. Reactions on the draft report were discussed and major decisions on the structure of the programme were taken. Faced with the realities of broad opposition against the draft plan within the faculty, it was more difficult to reach consensus. The main problem dealt with during the conference was the content of the proposed curriculum. The final report was written after this meeting and largely followed the line of thinking of the draft report. A major addition was a statement about the three pillars of the new curriculum: design, technology and research. The report also contained a chapter on implementation of the new plans. The consequences of developing a new programme within an existing faculty were outlined, including the need for teacher training, which would be provided by the department of educational research and development of the university of Limburg.

The Building Sciences PBL-curriculum

The PKB proposed a thematic structure for a two year common core program followed by gradual differentiation in the third year. In the fourth year students would specialize in one of the five areas of building sciences:
* A   Architecture
* B   Building technology
* M   Management and Administration
* P   Housing
* U   Urban design
The proposal for the Building Sciences PBL-curriculum was modelled after the Maastricht example. The six-week thematic block is taken as the standard programming unit. The choice of themes is derived from questions or problem areas of building sciences practice. The contributions from various disciplines are integrated in each block. Practical exercises and skills training (design) are linked to the theme of the block. Teams of teachers would be responsible to implement the block programmes in line with the proposed objectives.
The educational programme of each block is documented by means of a blockbook that has

to be approved in advance by a programme committee. The blockbook is not a syllabus or a reader, but rather study guide. The core of the blockbook consists of a series of 10-15 problem tasks, design assignments or cases. In two small-group meetings twice a week students analyze these tasks in order to formulate their learning goals. The basically self-steering learning process is guided by a tutor (a staff-member who supervises these meetings). More than 50% of the study time is reserved for independent study. A study center furnished with all sorts of learning resources (literature, video, etc.) is at the disposal of the students. The study activities are further sustained by a programme of design assignments, practice exercises, and occasionally lectures.

The twelve block themes of the first two years are ordered in a tile-like structure. Along the line students are systematically confronted with different scales of building (area, city, quarter, building, house, detail). As students move from one block to the next the content gradually becomes more complex.

Figure 1: Structure of the Building Sciences PBL curriculum

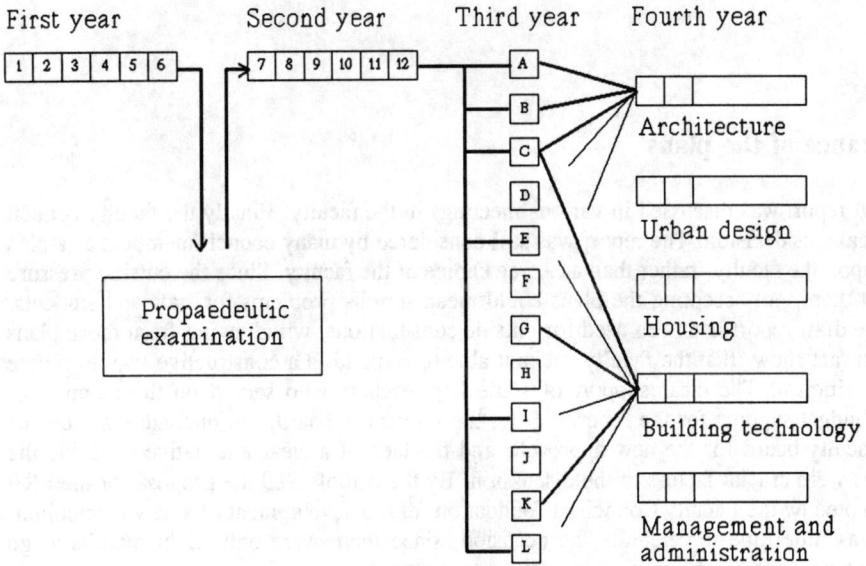

Figure 2: Thematic blocks of the first two years

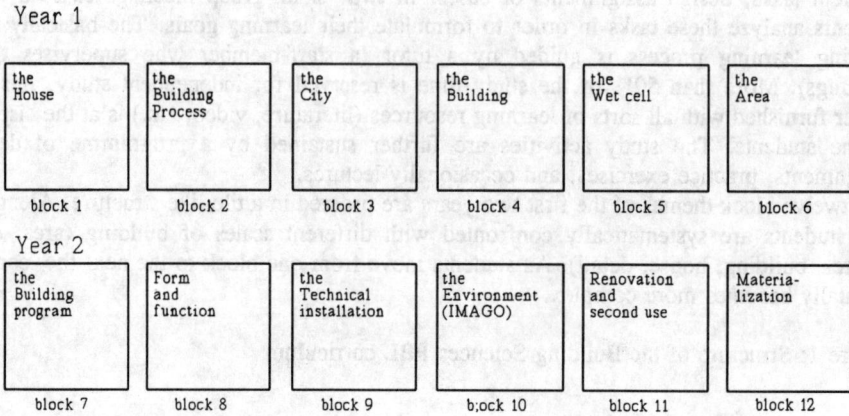

Year 1

the House	the Building Process	the City	the Building	the Wet cell	the Area
block 1	block 2	block 3	block 4	block 5	block 6

Year 2

the Building program	Form and function	the Technical installation	the Environment (IMAGO)	Renovation and second use	Materia- lization
block 7	block 8	block 9	b;ock 10	block 11	block 12

Acceptance of the plans

The final report was discussed in various meetings in the faculty. Finally the faculty council had to make its decision. The report was still considered by many council members as a plan forced upon the faculty, rather than as a free choice of the faculty. Since the outside pressure was still there, not accepting the plans could mean serious problems for staff and students. Since the draft report had been used for outside consultations, withdrawing from those plans would in fact show, that the faculty was not able to respond in a constructive way to severe outside criticism. The clear support of some key teachers who served on the committee, special budget support for the renewal from the university board, the unconditional choice of the faculty board for the new approach, and the lack of a clear alternative to tackle the problems were crucial factors in the discussion. By the end of 1989 the proposal of the PKB was accepted by the Faculty Council as foundation for the development of a new curriculum. There was little time to celebrate the occasion, since there were only eight months to go before the entering class would start in the new curriculum.

Arthur Levine (1980) in his study on change in American colleges concluded, that real change mostly occurred under external pressure. He also showed, that survival of innovation takes more than that. The Delft faculty of Building Sciences changed its course under severe pressure, but could it really make the changes needed? The innovators felt, that the formal acceptance of the plans was just one step in the renewal process. Unlike schools, who introduced PBL right from the start, a programme had to be developed within a large existing institution. Eight months after the decision of the council over 400 first-year students would start in a new curriculum, which was only briefly described in the final report. Although the policy of the faculty board was to phase out the existing curriculum and its organizational support structures as quickly as possible, it was inevitable that old and new structures would co-exist for some time. Moreover, the teaching staff would have to function in both

22

programmes for some time. The development of the new programme as a separate track with separated budgets and staff, an alternative strategy to introduce PBL in existing institutions (Kantrowitz et al. 1987), was impossible in view of the external pressure to change fast and unconditional. Under these circumstances a competition between the new developments and the existing programme was not inconceivable. In line with the recommendations of the report coordinators for the first year programme were appointed, a coordinating committee was appointed to monitor the implementation of the curriculum plans, faculty development programmes started, and additional staff was hired to support the new developments. The faculty board chose to raise the commitment of staff and students by stimulating wide participation in the implementation of the plans. Teacher training sessions were planned to introduce more staff to the educational strategies of the new curriculum. The foundation was laid for the construction of a new curriculum.

References

Bouhuijs, P.A.J., van der Vleuten, C., and van Luyk, S.J. (1987) The OSCE as a part of a systematic skills training approach. **Medical Teacher**, 9, 183-191, 1987.

Bouhuijs, P.A.J. (1990) Organizational and educational innovation. In: C. van der Vleuten & W. Wijnen (eds.) **Problem-based learning: perspectives from the Maastricht experience.** Amsterdam: Thesis publishers.

Engel, C.E. (1991). Not just a method but a way of learning. In D. Boud & G. Feletti (eds.), **The Challenge of Problem-based Learning.** London: Kogan Page.

De Graaff, E. and P. Frijns (1990) **Teacher roles in a Problem-based curriculum.** Paper presented at the Second International Symposium on Problem-based Learning, Yogyakarta, Indonesia, october 7-12, 1990.

Gijselaers W. (1990) **Curriculum evaluation.** In: C. van der Vleuten & W. Wijnen (eds.) **Problem-based learning: perspectives from the Maastricht experience.** Amsterdam: Thesis publishers.

Kantrowitz, M. et al. (1987) **Innovative tracks at established institutions for the education of health personnel.** WHO Offset publication No. 101. Geneva: World Health Organization.

Maitland, B. (1991). Problem-based learning for an architecture degree. In D. Boud & G. Feletti (eds.), **The Challenge of Problem-based Learning.** London: Kogan Page.

Moust, J.C.H., Bouhuijs, P.A.J. and Schmidt, H.G. (1989). **Probleemgestuurd leren** [Problem-based Learning]. Groningen: Wolters-Noordhoff.

Neufeld, V. & Barrows, H.S. (1974). The Mc Master Philosophy: An approach to medical education. **Journal of Medical Education**, 49, 1040-1050.

Programma Commissie Bouwkunde, PKB (1989). **Herprofilering van de Bouwkundeopleiding aan de Technische Universiteit Delft**; [A New Profile for Building Sciences at the TUD; Foundations of a new and braoadend educational programme]. Delft: Technische Universiteit Delft, Faculteit der Bouwkunde.

Post, G.J., De Graaff, E. and Drop, M.J. (1988) **Efficiency of a Primary-Care Curriculum.** Annals of Community-Oriented Education, 1, 25-31.

Statistisch jaarboek '88/'89 (1989). Delft: Technische Universiteit Delft, Bureau van de Universiteit.

Van Dalen, J. (1990) **Skillslab, a center for training of skills.** In: C. van der Vleuten & W. Wijnen (eds.) **Problem-based learning: perspectives from the Maastricht experience.** Amsterdam: Thesis publishers.

Van der Vleuten, C. & Verwijnen, M. (1990) A system for student assessment. In: C. van der Vleuten & W. Wijnen (eds.) **Problem-based learning: perspectives from the Maastricht experience.** Amsterdam: Thesis publishers.

Verkeningscommissie Bouwkunde (1989). **Eindrapportage** [Final Report].

Vernieuwingscommissie (1988) **Concentratie en Kristallisatie.** Delft: Technische Universiteit Delft, Faculteit der Bouwkunde.

chapter 3

The implementation of problem based learning at the Faculty of Building Sciences: management of educational change

Erik de Graaff & Peter A. J. Bouhuijs

Introduction

The implementation of a new curriculum is a complex operation, that affects all members of the staff. Especially when the introduction of a new educational approach like Problem Based learning PBL is involved, serious problems are to be expected (Schmidt, 1990). PBL is not just a set of new educational techniques, that the teaching staff can acquire in a few training sessions. It actually involves a completely different way of looking at the process of teaching and learning, and encompasses a change in attitude at the individual level and a culture change at the level of the institute. The integration of disciplines in a PBL-curriculum is not just a different way to arrange the educational programme. The breaking down of the borders between disciplines requires cooperation were there used to be competition among staff members.

At the same time, the traditional patterns of communication are uprooted. The old organizational structures are unsuitable to cope with the type of decisions that have to be made. Traditionally university teachers have a high degree of autonomy in choosing the educational format for their discipline. The university organization is characterized as a Professional Bureaucracy (Moen, 1989). Decisions at the central level (Faculty board and council) usually have a global nature, confirming the existing political equilibrium. Therefore, as part of the process of implementation of a PBL-curriculum new organizational structures need to be designed, that allow for central coordination of the educational programme.

Educational management is a crucial factor in curriculum innovation. Fullan quotes a deputy minister of education: "Well the hard work is done. We have the policy passed; now all you have to do is implement it", thereby ironically indicating that the real work only just begins when plans are accepted (Fullan, 1982, p. 54). Important tasks at the start of the implementation of the PBL-curriculum are: the professionalization of the staff, especially the training of tutorial skills, the development of study facilities for self-directed learning, the development of assessment methods in concordance with the demands of the problem-based curriculum and the design of a systematic approach to programme-evaluation. Management needs tools to implement these new policies.

In this chapter the implementation of PBL at the faculty of Building Sciences will be discussed from the perspective of innovation-management.

The choice for problem-based learning

The first step in educational innovation is a political one: the decision has to be made that something has to change. Literature on educational innovation invariably underscores the importance of careful preparation of decision-making (Fullan, 1982). Success stories of educational innovation are characterized by strong educational leadership. Consent should be gained by coercion rather than by force. If it is not possible to reach a unanimous decisions, at least consensus should be negotiated (Dalin, 1978).

In the case of Building Sciences the decision to change the curriculum was strongly motivated by external pressure (De Graaff & Van der Woord, 1990). A radical change of the educational programme was necessary in order to avoid worse alternatives, like the discontinuation of the Faculty or a forced merger with another school. There was relatively little time available and the reactions to the external pressure at the faculty were strongly divided, which made it impossible to get general acceptance for any proposal.

At general meetings members of the faculty severely criticized the PBL-curriculum proposed by the Programme Committee Building sciences (see: chapter 2). The decision of the Faculty Council to accept the proposal as foundation for the development of a new curriculum was not taken whole heartedly. Time was pressing and there simply were no alternatives. The procedure was compared to a "shotgun wedding".

At that time the Faculty Board turned the external pressure and the lack of time into momentum for change, using it deliberately to speed up the process. The new curriculum should be ready to receive the first students in little more than half a year. The main objective was to get the train moving. Directly after the acceptation of the PKB-proposal by the council a series of training sessions and workshops with the prospective members of the first blockgroups was organized. Participants were chosen by the faculty board in order to ensure that "major stakeholders" were included so that they could be committed to the development of the new curriculum (Grant and Gale, 1989). In the mean time, a new organization structure was build adjacent to the existing one.

The organizational structure of the PBL-curriculum

The traditional Faculty structure with rather autonomous discipline sections is not suited for decision on a thematic programme. In a PBL-curriculum decisions regarding educational issues need to be made above the level of the discipline and preferably below that of the Faculty board. As described in chapter 4 the faculty of Policy and administrative sciences in Nijmegen deals with the organizational problem by means of the university school concept. At the University of Limburg the problem is tackled by applying the principles of matrix-organization. The educational organization is build out of "educational projects" in which members of different discipline-sections participate. The faculty of Building Sciences developed a similar kind of matrix-organization.

At the top of the project structure the Faculty Board of Building Sciences installed the Implementation Committee Educational programme Building Sciences (ICOB). As an advisory committee to the board the ICOB was charged with the responsibility for the development of the new curriculum. Members of ICOB were selected on personal merit, rather than as representatives of any other body within the faculty.

Downward from ICOB a linking-pin structure was designed. Each ICOB-member was assigned a part of the curriculum (the first year, the second year and the graduation majors), chairing the respective curriculum-groups, consisting of the block-coordinators, which in turn chair their block-groups.

Figure 1: The organization structure of the PBL-curriculum

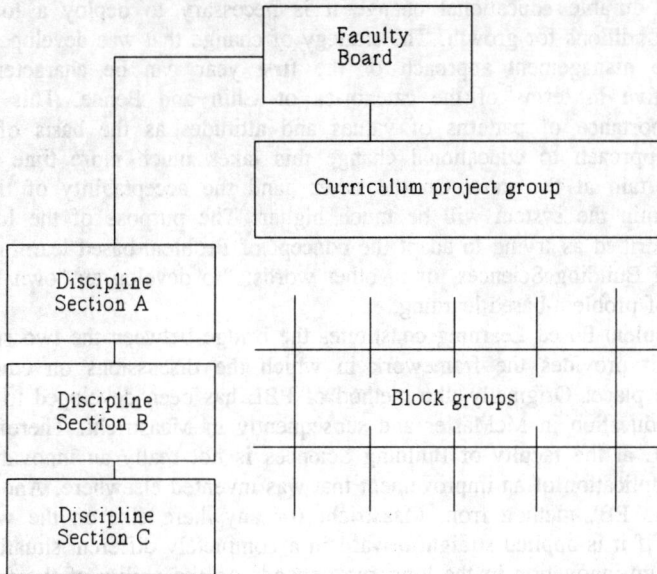

```
                    ┌──────────────┐
                    │   Faculty    │
                    │    Board     │
                    └──────────────┘
                           │
                    ┌─────────────────────────┐
                    │ Curriculum project group │
                    └─────────────────────────┘
       │
┌──────────────┐
│  Discipline  │
│  Section A   │
└──────────────┘
                    ┌──────────────┐
┌──────────────┐    │ Block groups │
│  Discipline  │    └──────────────┘
│  Section B   │
└──────────────┘
┌──────────────┐
│  Discipline  │
│  Section C   │
└──────────────┘
```

Management of change

The governing of a large institute like a university faculty is sometimes compared with the navigation of a super tanker. The inertia of the mass precludes an abrupt change of course. In other words, the operation of changing an organization involves strategic planning, with short term and long term goals. Chin and Benne (1985) distinguish three types of strategies that can be applied in changing an organization:
* Empirical-rational strategies
* Normative-re-educative strategies
* Power-coercive strategies

The top-down management style in the first phase of the implementation of PBL at Building Sciences can be characterized as a power-coercive approach. This strategy exercises formal power and primarily serves the immediate needs of quick visible results. Although, this strategy may be successful in solving the most urgent problems, it is recognized that the effects are limited in the long run.

The main disadvantage is that people who have been surpassed in the decision-making will have little reason to support the outcomes. Staff members who did not feel the need to dance to the tune of the outside critics naturally opposed the decision to embrace PBL. They are to be expected to reject the method as "not suitable for our needs" and "not invented here". When the objective is to effect educational change this opposition constitutes a serious problem. Support of the teaching staff is necessary, because they are the ones that will have to carry out the decisions. A major drawback of the power-coercive strategy, is that the initiative rests with a rather small group that can easily get isolated. This group may serve well to get the train in motion, but in order to sustain that motion, broad support among the staff is necessary.

In order to effect durable educational change it is necessary to deploy a long term strategy, creating conditions for growth. The strategy of change that was developed below the surface of the management approach of the first year can be characterized as normative-re-educative in terms of the categories of Chin and Benne. This strategy recognizes the importance of patterns of values and attitudes as the basis of human behavior. As an approach to educational change this takes much more time and the outcomes are uncertain at the start. On the other hand the acceptability of the ideas generated from within the system will be much higher. The purpose of the long-term strategy can be described as trying to adapt the concept of Problem-based learning to the specific situation of Building Sciences, or in other words: "to develop an "own Building Sciences version" of problem-based learning.

The concept of Problem-Based Learning constitutes the bridge between the two strategies in the sense that it provides the framework in which the discussions on educational innovation can take place. Originally, the method of PBL has been developed to suit the needs of medical education in McMaster and subsequently in Maastricht. Therefore, the introduction of PBL at the faculty of Building Sciences is not really an innovation, but indeed rather the application of an improvement that was invented elsewhere. And even as an improvement the PBL-method from Maastricht (or anywhere else on the world) is bound to fall short if it is applied straightforward in a completely different situation. The success of curriculum-innovation in the long run depends on the ability of the faculty to adapt the educational method to suit its own specific needs. In order to be truly innovative the new curriculum should result in increased competence for the organization and its members (De Zeeuw, 1990).

An important advantage of the introduction of PBL is that it entails a new way of thinking about education and learning. In the old situation there was little need for reflection on the task of teaching. Discussion on education was mostly confined within the disciplinary boundaries. The PBL-curriculum breaks down these traditional boundaries. Discussions on the educational approach are further encouraged by the availability of detailed educational programmes (the blockbooks). At a conference in february 1992 the Faculty Board explicitly emphasized the importance of continuous improvement of the educational method in the course of adaptation to the needs of Building Sciences. The installation of an educational unit within the faculty is an important factor in the strategy of ongoing innovation, embodying the systematic approach to educational development, programme evaluation and faculty development.

Human Resources Management

An important goal for the educational innovation at Building Sciences is the development an organization structure which enables the professionalization of the teaching staff. The ultimate goal of educational change is learning new ways of thinking and doing: new knowledge, skills and attitudes. Therefore, it follows that staff development is one of the most important factors related to change in practice (Fullan, 1982, p.66). University teachers are qualified specialists. Within the framework of the professional bureaucracy the competency of faculty members is primarily defined in terms of experience in the field and discipline expertise. Educational performance is of little consequence. Measured against these criteria, interdisciplinary competence gain is bound to go unnoticed. Consequently competence must be redefined, both at an individual level, as at the level of the institute.

In the matrix organization the responsibility for educational issues is located in the project structure. Within this structure the guiding educational principles are centrally defined. The paradigm of Human Resources Management (HRM) appears suited to enforce these developments. With respect to organizational innovation HRM stresses the importance of the human capital, with a central position for the selection, allocation and training of faculty (Vloeberghs, 1989). Tailored training programmes constitute an important element in the long term strategy of innovation. The purpose is to gradually reevaluate the staff and provide opportunities for further personal development in order to attain a more flexible educational organization. Together with the approach of ongoing innovation this should result in increased competence for the institution as well as its members

References

Chin, R. & Benne, K.D. (1985). General strategies for effecting changes in human systems. In W.G. Bennis, K.D. Benne & R. Chin, **The planning of change** (fourth edition). New York: Holt, Rinehart & Winston.

Dalin, P. (1978) **Limits to educational change.** London: Macmillan.

De Graaff, E. & Van der Woord, J. (1990). Changing horses mid-course. Paper presented at the Second International Symposium on Problem-Based Learning, Yogyakarta. Indonesia October 7-12-1990.

Fullan, M. (1982). **The Meaning of Educational Change.** New York/London: Teachers College, Columbia University.

Grant, J. & Gale, R. (1989) Changing Medical Education. **Medical Education,** 23, 252-257.

Moen, J. (1989) **Innoveren in universitair onderwijs; Organisatie- en** curriculumontwikkeling in een nieuwe universitaire opleiding. 's-Gravenhage: VUGA.

Schmidt, H.G. (1990) Onderwijskundige aspekten van probleemgestuurd onderwijs. In W.S. Jochems (red.), **Activerend Onderwijs, over onderwijsvormen die het leren bevorderen** [Activating Education, on educational formats that encourage learning]. Delft: Delft Universitaire pers.

Vloeberghs, D. (1989). **Human Resources Management.** Leuven/Amersfoort: Acco.

De Zeeuw. G. (1990). Problemen van verbeteren en innoveren [Problems of improvement and innovation]. In: **Postdoctorale opleiding Innovatie manager.** Amsterdam: Academie voor Informatica, Universiteit van Amsterdam.

chapter 4

The introduction of problem-based learning in the Faculty of Policy and Administrative Sciences: a management approach

Herman van den Bosch & Wim H. Gijselaers

Introduction

Problem-based learning (PBL) is regarded as a valuable attempt to improve the quality of higher education (Schmidt & de Volder, 1984). It is an innovative instructional method presenting various theories as an instrument to understand and explain problems. Since 1988, the Faculty of Policy and Administration Sciences (FPAS) of the University of Nijmegen (the Netherlands) has pioneered a curriculum based on problem-based learning. The principal idea is, that learning should be organized around problems which are related to the profession, rather than around subjects which are centered around academic disciplines. Considerable efforts have been made by this faculty to design a curriculum and employ innovative teaching methods which intend to achieve multi- or interdisciplinary education, to encourage self-directed learning, and to provide students with an adequate background to analyze problems encountered in the professions of policy and administrative sciences.

This contribution seeks to describe the process through which the faculty became aware of the need to develop new ideas in teaching (in particular problem-based learning), adopt or reject them, and to institutionalize these ideas.

The Faculty of Policy and Administrative Sciences

The Faculty of Policy and Administrative Sciences (FPAS) is the result of a merger in 1988 between several established faculties, departments, institutions and programmes concerning policy and administrative sciences. The creation of this faculty was a response to changes in societal need (society wanted graduates trained in various aspects of policy and administrative sciences) and to external pressures (a serious decline in student enrolment for some programmes in policy sciences combined with lower budgets).

External pressure and 'culture management'

External pressure and internal culture management serve both as antagonist as well as mutual supportive conditions. Many innovations in university institutions are the result of external pressure (for example, negative judgments of external review committees, decreases in student enrolment or in governmental financial support. External pressure also played a decisive role in the curriculum innovation of the FPAS. The decision in favor of a new curriculum in which PBL was to play a major role, was made in a period when FPAS had interim management. The University of Nijmegen introduced interim management for FPAS because of earlier problems with the existing programmes and problems raised as a result of the fusion. Teachers were compelled by the interim management to accept PBL as new teaching method. Teacher training was obligatory for staff members to learn the basic principles of PBL. From a perspective of university organizations, this is an unusual and unconventional process of decision-making. However, this didn't result in protests or faculty dissent. A great number of staff members realized that the possibility to keep their jobs depended largely on the increasing amount of student enrolment, due to the attractiveness of the new programme.

Innovations characterized as 'threat-response' will only last as long as the threatening conditions are present or can be cultivated. If a decision-making approach still continues to be top-down in the long term, staff members will not feel responsible for the transfer of the innovations. They hide in their research activities or frustrate the entire process. In a university with its typical vague hierarchical structure, staff members have nearly unrestricted possibilities to follow their own preferences or to minimize efforts in realizing faculty based goals.

For all this reasons management of he FPAS had to make great efforts to get support from staff members, not based on coercion but on shared values. Staff members are required to see that the innovations are not only necessary adaptations to external pressures, but may have values in their own right. Because of proceeding in this line, a considerable number of staff members started considering innovations as a challenge and an opportunity to promote the institution, and to a certain degree also themselves. Of course, as long as people behave in a rational way, innovations cannot be 'sold' as toothbrushes. Educational innovations in a university context have to be as convincing as research activities. Educational qualities of innovations need to prove that they are worthwhile. In this respect, the presence of 'models', for example other university institutions that can be characterized as successful adapters, is not without importance. Models can be considered as successful, when their more superficial aspects are rejected and replaced by home-made modifications.

Outline of a new programme
The new programme consists of four years divided into two cycles. The first cycle (year one and two) contains a broad introduction in policy and administrative sciences. These years are organized around courses with central themes from these sciences. They have a multidisciplinary orientation. The second cycle, the final two years, comprises courses with a more disciplinary character. The management of the programme follows the structure of the curriculum. The first cycle is embedded and coordinated by a relatively autonomous institution called 'School for policy and administrative sciences'. The second cycle is organized by the individual departments of the faculty.

Analytical frameworks for innovation and change in Higher Education

Classical innovation theory heavily relies on the idea of stages or phases in innovations: adoption, implementation, dissemination (Hill & Friedman, 1979; Kozma, 1985). However, Kozma (1985) showed that a considerable overlap and ambiguity exist between these stages, and that innovation is evolutionary (new instructional practices are built on past practices). According to Kozma these stages are not easily to distinguish. A clear point of adoption or implementation is rarely discernible. This seems indicative for the most characteristic aspect of instructional innovation: new educational practices are based on past practices. Whenever instructors employ new teaching methods, these methods are embedded in earlier teaching experiences.

An obvious question is which conditions have a major influence on innovation processes. Literature on change and innovation suggests that the most pervasive factor is the unique organizational structure of higher education (Bess, 1984; Kozma, 1985). Kozma (1985) points out that academic organizations are characterized by their perpetual inability to strike a wholly satisfactorily balance between the requirements for individual autonomy and academic freedom on the one hand, and the necessity for organizational efficiency, accountability and control on the other hand. The organizational looseness, or lack of instructional accountability, accounts for the personal character of many innovations in higher education. Dependence on a variety of personal preferences of instructors leads to unclear choices in decision processes. Innovations outreaching the level of individual instructors, for example rearrangement of course contents at a programme level, are particularly vulnerable for failure and resistance to change. At a programme level it is difficult to operate on a basis of a variety of individual, and therefore inconsistent, preferences that can be described better as a loose collection of ideas than a coherent structure (Cohen, March & Olsen, 1972).

A second condition is external pressure (Lindquist, 1978). Declining student enrolment, external reviews, changes in higher education policy and finance, changes in public expectations, are generally seen as relevant external forces. Innovations are apt to occur whenever these external forces grow stronger. They are more important than internal forces to invoke educational change.

A third condition is funding or the availability of additional resources. Innovations require time and or other resources. Lack of resources, as Kozma (1985) points out, is one of the most frequently given reasons for not adopting an innovation. Instructional change is only possible if change doesn't cost anything. When costs are incurred, faculty members have to spent time on obtaining additional resources. These activities undermine the possibility for following individual preferences that make part of the goals set in the academic career. Individual preferences normally lie in the field of research. Research activities are the most rewarding activities in an academic career. Implementing innovations in education implies that faculty members have to undertake activities that are not perceived as a valuable contribution to their own career. Consequently a feeling of being hindered by educational innovations in the pursuit of academic career will emerge which ultimately leads to rejection or non adoption of new ideas (Oldham & Kulik, 1984).

The analytical framework as described above leads to several practical implications. First, powerful management is needed to create coherent structures in a faculty. Coherent concerning the intended educational goals, methods and evaluation and assessment. Second, external pressure is needed to legitimize the actions undertaken by the management. External pressure provides management a basis to change the balance between individual autonomy and faculty control in the favor of faculty control. Finally, management should try to use external pressure for adopting new ideas and to create a faculty wide approval (corporate identity). This part of management decisions may be described as "culture" management: management of affective goals which influence the culture within a faculty in favor of willing to change education. Normally management decisions focus on organizational structure variables (funding, roles and functions of departments).

33

Because of the overwhelming importance of the first of the above mentioned implications - powerful management - the FPAS introduces the 'University School' as organizational principle. In the next section we make some remarks about the appropriateness of the School concept.

The 'University school' as organizational principle

In our discussion about the school concept we differentiate between three aspects:
* the School as an organizational entity
* the School as an institution
* the School as a focus of innovation

Organizational entity
The school concept is related with the idea of project teams ex article 40 according to the Dutch law on higher education. Daily co-ordination of the programme is done by a programme director and his staff. A council provides the director with complimentary advises and ensures the quality of the programme.
The foundation of an autonomous entity was motivated by the necessity to guarantee a comprehensive curriculum in an environment that was characterized by antagonism and heterogeneity. In fact, this situation turned out to be a matrix organization, entailing its characteristic possibilities and problems. The relative simple recruitment of teaching staff can be considered as an advantage: faculty members spend their time in their own divisions and in the School. Problems may occur when staff members identify themselves mostly with their own divisions. Nowadays, 30 percent of the total staff of the School is a full-time member of the School staff. These members have specific tasks as communication trainers, tutors or laboratory assistants.

Institution
The School is responsible for about 1000 students. For this group it operates as a professional organization: it organizes the curriculum, including the examinations, registers the students, and gives information to potential students. A support staff of 10 persons is employed to achieve these goals.
The student library ('study landscape') constitutes a major element of the equipment of the School. Here, students find the necessary literature, personal computers and video-recorders. The student library and its adjacent territories function as a meeting place for the students. Although the place is sometimes heavily crowded, students find enough room for intellectual and for social activities.

Focus of innovation
Without the presence of a School, the development of a coherent programme in the first cycle had probably not been possible. This programme is based on the principles of problem-based learning: multidisciplinary oriented courses and small group tutorials. The choice for problem-based learning as principal instructional method was a top-down decision. The management of the School was equipped with enough power to introduce a number of supportive activities, like compulsory training, participation in programme committees, new roles in teaching etcetera. At the same time, the distance between the

34

management of the School and the teaching staff was small enough to discuss the innovations and even to modify them, in the case of important resistance. The presence of the School also facilitates research about the learning activities of the students.

Merits of the concept 'University school'

The foundation of a university school could be desirable when one or more of the three following conditions apply:
* a specific programme lacks a clear organizational structure; for instance: several departments share their responsibility for a programme
* a unifying philosophy of education needs to be developed
* a professional organizational entity is needed.

However, the concept of a university school has many aspects and each aspect has it's own variants. We'll discuss these aspects and variants in the following.

Delegation of power

To prevent school management from being a paper tiger and just fulfil the role of another piece of university bureaucracy, existing organizational entities (faculty, departments, disciplinary sections) must delegate power to the school management. In addition clear definitions must exist about the role the school may play within a faculty organization. The FPAS has good experiences with installing a director having responsibility for daily affairs and a board, responsible for the long term policy. The units or departments that delegated power to the School are represented in the board.

Delegation of staff

To operate in an efficient way, and to prevent competence conflicts with other units within a faculty, financial resources needed for teaching- and organizational activities should be allocated to the School. Having an own budget available, the School negotiates with the disciplinary sections in the faculty to obtain educational expertise. Of course, this practice requires an adequate description and accounting of teaching tasks. The FPAS has developed an extensive 'credit list' of required teaching-tasks and teaching roles. The budget of the School and the prices are defined in hours of teaching load. For example: a lecture taking place for one hour is credited as 4 hours teaching load; a tutorial amounts to 50 hours teaching load. Consequently, many university teachers participate in the School programme to gain enough credit hours.

School management prefers a situation having a restricted number of department members available, above the participation of many staff members for only a small part of credit hours. Continuity and educational quality is best served by a small amount of staff members performing a relatively large amount of teaching roles.

Professionalism

A School doesn't need its own teaching-staff, except for highly specialized tasks. The School of FPAS for instance, employs specialists in gender studies, philosophy of policy and administrative sciences and in communication skills. Student administration, informational and other student services, as well curriculum and organizational expertise, and teacher training facilities are necessary within the School.

Quality management

A School has to implement a quality management system: all courses and the curriculum as such should be evaluated periodically. A discussion of evaluation outcomes should be standard routine within the board. Evaluation results are useful to improve educational quality, or provide teachers with opportunities to improve their teaching skills. Teachers who persist in not being successful in performing certain teaching activities may be replaced, or get other teaching roles. A such quality management is needed to assure educational quality and to obtain information for accountability purposes.

Conclusion

It is often thought that only new schools can implement PBL because of the radical changes needed in the organizational structure (Bouhuijs, 1990). The case described in this article proves that under certain conditions PBL can also be introduced in established faculties. In this particular case the explicit attention for management issues (for example, introduction of the school concept and culture management) facilitated the introduction of PBL.

Two other conditions appeared also to be of importance: The first condition is that external pressures are strong enough, in combination with changed management procedures, to provide adequate resistance to internal forces wanting no change. The second condition is that attention was paid to faculty approval and organizational culture. Management tried to change the organizational culture by explicitly focusing attention to compliance with the programme. For example, staff members were schooled in the principles of PBL at the University of Limburg. However, as such the management of FPAS has the feeling that when looking back into the past period even more attention should have been paid to cultural changes. More seminars, courses, workshop, internal magazines, festivities, financial stimuli to reward wanted organizational behavior, should have been organized. Last but not least, student involvement and participation in the management of the programme is needed to support the process of change.

References

Barrows, H.S. & Tamblyn, R.M. (1980) **Problem-Based Learning: an Approach to Medical Education** New York: Springer Publishing Company.

Bouhuijs, P.A.J. (1990). **The maintenance of educational innovations in medical schools.** In: Nooman, Z.M., Schmidt, H.G., & Ezzat, E.S. Innovation in medical education. New York: Springer Publishing Company (pp. 175 - 188).

Cohen, M.D., March, J.G., & Olsen, J.P. (1972). A garbage can model of Organizational Choice. **Administrative Science Quarterly**, 17, 1 - 25.

Goodlad, S. (Ed) (1984) **Education for the Professions.** Quis custodiet? Guildford Surrey: SRHE & NFER-NELSON.

Hill, D.D. & Friedman, C.P. (1979). An analysis of frameworks for research on innovation and change in higher education. **Review of Educational Research**, 49, 411-435.

Kozma, R.B. (1985). A grounded theory of instructional innovation in higher education. **Journal of Higher Education**, 56, 300-319.

Lindquist, J. (1979). **Strategies for change**. Richardson, CA: Pacific Sounding Press.

Oldham, G.R., & Kulik, C.T. (1984). Motivation enhancement through work redesign. In Bess, J.L. (Ed.). **College and University Organization.** New York: University Press.

Schmidt, H.G., & de Volder, M.L. (Eds) (1984) **Tutorials in Problem-Based Learning.** A New Direction in Teaching the Health Professions Assen: Van Gorcum.

Part II

Consequences of the Introduction

of a PBL-curriculum

chapter 5

How to turn teachers into facilitators of the learning processes
- Staff Development as a tool in the Implementation of Educational Innovation

Jan van Driel[1]

"The most influential factor in educational change is the teacher."
(Duffee & Aikenhead, 1992)

Introduction

Research in the field of curriculum innovation always shows that innovations introducing changes in the way of teaching can only be successful if teachers actually succeed in performing the desired teaching skills. The statement quoted from Duffee and Aikenhead is only one example to illustrate the crucial role of teachers in this respect. In their article they argue on the basis of a literature survey that teachers use their own so-called 'practical knowledge' to make decisions on all aspects of teaching. This practical knowledge may consist of cause-effect propositions from many sources, rules of thumb as well as generalizations drawn from personal experiences, beliefs, values and prejudices. In the context of curriculum innovation three components of teacher practical knowledge appear to be important: (1) teachers' past experiences (including formal education); (2) teachers' current teaching situation; and (3) teachers' visions of what teaching should be like. They emphasize that teacher practical knowledge is strongly influenced by personal beliefs and values that are quite often deeply rooted and therefore resistant to change (Duffee & Aikenhead, 1992).

Tobin and Dawson (1992) largely attribute the relative lack of success in numerous curriculum reform efforts to the (often tacit) assumption that a curriculum is independent of instruction. Tobin and Dawson argue that when an attempt is made to change a curriculum, not only teaching staff and students should be taken into account, but also the culture in which the curriculum is to be embedded. If a change of curriculum introduces teaching practices that are considered taboo within the culture, there is little chance that teachers will use or incorporate these practices in the intended way.

The implementation of a problem-based curriculum in an existing educational environment places great demands in this respect: teachers do not only need to acquire specific teaching skills, but they are also required to adopt a specific attitude towards teaching (Schmidt, 1990; Todd, 1991). This attitude differs from those that currently occur in higher education. In short this involves a shift from teacher-centered education, in which the teacher is the professional expert who 'transfers his knowledge upon the students', to self-directed learning. In the latter view the teacher is considered to be a facilitator of learning processes: he stimulates and supports students who are actively engaged in obtaining knowledge and skills.

---

[1] Acknowledgement: The author wishes to thank ms. Diana Vinke of the Delft University of Technology for her help with the translation and comment on the manuscript of this paper.

41

Taking the case of Building Sciences at Delft University of Technology as an example, this paper describes a way of staff development connected with the implementation of a problem-based curriculum, including results that were obtained with the approach chosen. Finally conclusions with respect to the future will be drawn. First however, some information is given on specific tasks of teaching staff in a problem-based curriculum.

Specific tasks of teaching staff in a problem-based curriculum

When the Faculty of Building Sciences in Delft chose to implement a problem-based curriculum, it was clear from the start that at least two specific tasks for teaching staff were to be introduced (De Graaff & Frijns, 1990). First, block planning groups were formed in order to develop multidisciplinary, thematic blocks. *Block planning groups* include teachers representing the different disciplines present in the block. Working in a team, these teachers first had to formulate learning objectives. They had to select subjectmatter and adequate instructional materials and methods and they had to construct study assignments, cases and tasks. All this should fit within the framework of problem-based learning (PBL). When they started, most block planning group members knew little of PBL, nor did they have any experience in designing PBL-blocks and in making an educational design within a team.

Secondly, the teachers had to perform as *tutors*. The main task of the tutor is to support the students learning. In this respect, the tutor teaches the students to handle problems systematically, to formulate adequate learning objectives and to report orally in a brief and well-structured way. The tutor also stimulates self-study activities by discussing questions such as 'how can certain knowledge be found?' and 'how can it be studied efficiently?'. From this description it should be clear that a tutor needs specific skills, which can be described as 'scientific' in a general sense. Also, and maybe more importantly, a certain attitude towards teaching is necessary. This attitude, which is consistent with a constructivist view of knowledge rather then an objectivist view, does not appear to have widespread acceptance amongst teachers (Tobin & Dawson, 1992).

Apart from this, a tutor also needs domain-specific knowledge in a broad sense: he must have an overview of the different disciplines present in the block and of their mutual relations. This does not imply, however, that he will have to explain or 'lecture' on subject matter[2]. Instead a tutor can give examples from professional practice in order to stimulate discussions and to get students enthusiastic about the topic or case under consideration.

---

[2]In many cases the tutor will not even be able to give a detailed explanation, considering the multidisciplinary nature of the blocks. Therefore the curriculum also contains lectures by professional experts on specific topics. Besides, students can consult teachers who are experts in specific fields and whose names and phone numbers are mentioned in the blockbooks.

Teacher training activities preceding the implementation of the new curriculum

Organizational aspects

It was decided by the board of the Faculty of Building Sciences that future block planning group members and tutors should be prepared for their new tasks by means of a training programme. Block planning group members had to participate in two conferences, followed by a tutorial training module of two days. The latter was also presented to future tutors. In fact, all faculty staff with an educational task were obliged to participate in this training module. In the months preceding the start of the actual implementation of the new curriculum all teaching staff were invited to participate in the course. A time schedule was designed in order to train the staff, arranged in groups of 8-12.

Eventually, about 15 groups participated in the two-day training session. The aim of training all faculty staff before the new curriculum started, was not completely achieved however. About one third of the staff cancelled or simply ignored the invitation to take the course.

In order to train these teachers all the same, as well as staff members who were appointed after the start of the new curriculum, a new series of training sessions was organized during the first year of the implementation. Eventually about 20% of the staff members never took this tutorial training course: some kept ignoring invitation upon invitation, others refused explicitly. Although the faculty board did not officially change their policy, they gave up putting pressure on these staff members.

Objectives

The conferences aimed at familiarizing staff with the principles of PBL and the premises of the new curriculum to be implemented. Therefore lectures, given by experts in the PBL-field who were invited as external consultants, as well as discussion sessions were included. In addition, workshop-like sessions were included in order to start with the design of the new curriculum.

The main purpose of the two-day tutorial training module was to practice tutorial skills. Therefore, the training module consisted for a large part of exercises. Arranged in groups of 8-12, participants simulated tutorial groups. They discussed cases, acting as though they were a group of students with one of them performing the role of tutor. In addition, videofragments of tutorial groups were used to demonstrate and discuss tutorial skills.

Training effects on block planning group members

The most important outcome of the conferences was that they helped to create an atmosphere in which future block planning group members were willing to work together in a team designing and developing the blocks. The conferences also showed that the principles and premises of a problem-based curriculum were far from self-evident for faculty staff. Ample discussions promoted understanding however.

The conferences did not fully succeed in teaching block planning group members how to design a block (e.g. how to connect subject matter with instructional formats), how to write cases, etc. The tutorial training module proved to be useful in this respect. This course offers an intensive confrontation with the way PBL 'works' at the micro-level of teaching. From this experience block planning group members gained insight and ideas with respect to the design of their blocks ('Now we know what PBL really looks like').

Training effects on other teaching staff

Teaching staff who had not participated in the conferences had to attend the tutorial training course. For them this course mainly served as an introduction to PBL. Especially in the first training groups, the simulation exercises led to profound discussions concerning the pros and cons of the educational system to be implemented. This partially prevented however tutorial skills from being practiced, which was the main purpose of the course.

On the basis of this evaluation, the training module was modified for later groups. More information (both oral and written) about PBL was included. The purpose of this modification was to make a distinction between information and opinions about PBL on the one hand, and practicing tutorial skills via simulation exercises on the other hand.

When entering the training module, most participants had a skeptical attitude. Many felt threatened by the curriculum innovation and the majority were not convinced that the choice for PBL was a right one. During the evaluation, at the end of the course the attitude of the majority of the participants towards PBL appeared to have changed from skeptical to moderately positive. Participants made remarks such as 'PBL contains promising aspects, though adaptations for building sciences will be necessary'; 'now I know more about the philosophy behind PBL, I'm more convinced of its strengths', etc.

Despite these positive outcomes, the training module failed with respect to its original purpose. During the evaluation, many participants appeared to regret that the two-day course had offered little opportunity to practice tutorial skills. Some of them felt that they needed more practicing in order to be capable of performing as a tutor.

Practical experiences with the new curriculum

Shortly after the start of the new curriculum in September 1990 problems of various nature arose. Most of these problems were indicated by the response to questionnaires, which were distributed after every block period amongst both teachers and students in order to evaluate the block (see chapter 6). One type of problems was related to *imperfections in the blocks*. Most blocks appeared to suffer from a lack of internal coherence and to be overloaded. The latter, in turn, resulted in too high a workload for students. Moreover inadequate instructional materials had been selected, inappropriate cases had been included, etc.

From the questionnaires it also became clear that in most tutorial groups the discussion of 'cases' was chaotic. Besides, *most students appeared to visit the tutorial group meetings badly prepared*, i.e. they had spent far too little time on self-study activities according to the learning objectives that had been formulated during the previous meeting. As a result, discussions of the results from self-study activities were poor, if they took place at all.

These problems can partly be explained by the fact that the students, most of whom directly came from secondary school, were not yet accommodated to studying in a problem-based curriculum. The Faculty of Building Sciences had underestimated its duty in this respect, since it had not paid enough attention to a careful and thorough introduction of students to the specific characteristics of the curriculum. But *these problems also relate directly to the performance of the tutors*. After all, it was their task to stimulate well-structured discussions and self-study activities.

Teacher training activities during the implementation of the new curriculum

A new series of 8 two-day tutorial training courses took place during the first year of implementation. As mentioned in section 3.1, this was necessary in order to train all faculty staff (present staff as well as new staff members). Apart from this, two other activities in the field of teacher training took place in the same period.

Organizational aspects

Beforehand it was decided to offer block-specific training by organizing *weekly teacher meetings* before and during the six weeks in which a block takes place. These meetings were visited by only half of the teachers (at the most). This fact can be explained in terms of a lack of involvement. Moreover, many remarks from teachers during these meetings indicated resistance to the role of tutor. It seemed that the premises of the tutor-role conflicted with the personal beliefs and concepts of teaching of many a staff member.

In order to tackle these problems, it was decided to organize *workshops* after every block for all staff members concerned. In order to obtain a maximal attendance all potential participants were addressed personally. In addition to evaluation, aimed at improving the blocks, these workshops were also meant to get staff members more acquainted with the new teacher roles. Therefore experiences and problems from educational practice were exchanged and discussed. To emphasize this aspect, the workshops were organized and conducted by a teacher trainer. Although participants were enthusiastic about these meetings, the large non-response (ca. 50%) was considered problematic.

Outcomes of the workshops

The workshops allowed a better understanding of the problems described above. For example, the striking fact that students prepared badly for their tutorial group meetings could be explained as the result of several factors. Some of these had to do with the poor quality of the 'cases' and/or the instructional materials selected. Besides, the combination of tutorial group meetings and self-study activities suffered from an informal organization, i.e. students were not obliged to participate in the meetings nor did the tutor assess in any way their activities during the meetings and/or their self-study activities. At the same time, the curriculum also contained design exercises. These were assessed by the design studio teachers on a weekly basis! In this context, one can hardly blame tutors for not being able to stimulate the students to prepare well for their tutorial group meetings.

Apart from this excuse, it was also clear that *many tutors proved to be incapable of teaching the process skills* mentioned in section 2. It is suggested that these teachers have not developed these skills fully themselves. Todd (1991) also experienced this problem when trying to prepare tertiary teachers for problem-based learning. She argues that if teachers feel inadequate, "they may not put enough emphasis on the students developing and practicing these important processes" (Todd, 1991).

The workshops also promoted insight into resistance of teachers to the tutor-role. This appeared above all to be caused by a loss of autonomy that teachers experienced on different levels:

* Tutors have to function within the framework of an educational system that was chosen by the board of the Faculty. The majority of the staff felt overtaken by this choice, which was not based upon a consultation of their opinion. In the existing educational

system, teachers had more freedom to choose educational methods and teaching aids according to their own opinions.
* Tutors have to function within a block which they did not design themselves, whereas they were used to a situation in which they were more or less autonomous with respect to the choice of subject-matter (both topics and sequence), instructional materials, problems, study tasks, exercises, and ways of testing and assessing the students.
* At the micro level of teaching, tutors experienced a loss of control and authority. Compared to the situation of teacher-centered instruction, where they are in control and are respected by the students for their knowledge and experience, many feel unsatisfied in a tutorial group which draws heavily on student responsibility. Todd (1991) considers this factor "by far the major difficulty" for teachers who had chosen to implement problem-based learning.

Conclusions

From the preceding description the following conclusions are drawn. Until this day, *a relatively large part of faculty staff keeps resisting to (specific aspects of) the curriculum innovation*. Some have succeeded to remain uninvolved with the implementation of the new curriculum. This fact can partly be explained by the way the implementation process was managed: faculty staff was hardly involved with and badly informed about this process (see chapter 3). In other words, this case provides another example of curriculum innovation in which the importance of the culture in which the new curriculum is to be embedded is underestimated.
Another explanation deals with the inconsistent and informal approach of the faculty board: although training sessions were intended to be obligatory, teachers could refuse to participate without any consequences. In general, block group planning members proved to be amongst the most motivated of faculty staff. The curriculum innovation has offered them tasks that stimulate their feeling of responsibility. Many of them experience a challenge in trying to develop a form of PBL that is adequate for university education in the building sciences. This cannot prevent however, that until today they make many mistakes in constructing the blocks. Additional training opportunities for block planning group members were offered, such as courses on how to construct cases, how to write test questions, etc. However, the faculty board considered these as unnecessary. In their view, practical experiences will teach block planning group members to improve in these respects.

With respect to the problems of individual tutors, it is useful to refer to a statement in section 1: it is necessary to change the attitude towards teaching of teachers when a PBL curriculum is to be implemented. Moreover, such a change must take place in order to allow new teaching skills to be learned. Because the faculty board had failed to inform and to motivate faculty staff beforehand, the two-day tutorial training course was inevitably devoted to aspects dealing mostly with attitude (information, discussion, motivation). Therefore, *the training of tutorial skills remained insufficient*. Moreover, most tutors could not benefit from practical experiences, since this was hindered by the problems mentioned in sections 4 and 5.2.

46

Further developments and recommendations

In order to solve motivational (and other) problems, the faculty board has chosen *to combine the tutor role with that of a design studio teacher*. This was mainly done in order to extend the job of a teacher with skills relating to professional expertise in a more familiar way and to increase the responsibility of teaching staff: in their role as design studio teachers they have the 'power' to assess students, which they lack when they are 'merely' a tutor. Anyway, being not only a tutor but also a design studio teacher enhances status amongst colleagues.

Apart from this the faculty board is advised to invest in additional forms of permanent in-service training, such as:
* Block-specific courses (on both subject-matter and teaching skills).
* Workshops and/or follow-up meetings on general themes (e.g. methodology of research and design, problem-solving, group dynamics, etc.). Todd (1991) reports positive outcomes of such workshops.
* Training at the micro level of education. For example mentoring by a teacher trainer and/or peer coaching (teachers visiting each others tutorial groups, followed by feedback sessions). A description of these techniques is, amongst others, given by Parker (1990).

The latter ways of staff development appear to be the most powerful, especially when applied to situations in which experienced teachers are asked to adopt new teaching behavior (Van der Vegt & Houtveen, 1992). Therefore the Faculty of Building Sciences is recommended to invest in these ways of staff development, rather then in another series of one-off training activities.

Activities considered desirable by the faculty should preferably be embedded within *a system of permanent staff development, to be integrated with staff management and organizational management*. Staff management should be aimed at deploying teachers as much as possible in blocks and in roles according to their affinity and in ways that stimulate their feeling of responsibility.

The main purpose of this set of activities should not only be to increase the expertise and the teaching skills of the staff, but also (and maybe most important) the motivation of the staff. For if an educational system requires teachers in the first place to be stimulators of learning activities, then motivated teachers are an inevitable condition.

References

Duffee, L., & Aikenhead, G. (1992). Curriculum Change, Student Evaluation, and Teacher Practical Knowledge. **Science Education**, 76, 493-506.

Graaff, E. de, & Frijns, P.H.A.M. (1990, October). Teacher Roles in a Problem Based Curriculum. Paper presented at **the 2nd International Symposium on Problem-Based Learning**, Yogyakarta, Indonesia.

Parker, L.S. (1990). A Prototypic Human Resource Model. In P. Burke, R. Heidemann & C. Heidemann (Eds.), **Programming for Staff Development: Fanning the Flame** (pp. 87-116). London: The Falmer Press.

Schmidt, H.G. (1990). Onderwijskundige Aspecten van Probleemgestuurd Onderwijs [Educational Aspects of Problem Based Learning]. In W.M.G. Jochems (Ed.), **Verslag Symposium Aktiverend Onderwijs** (pp. 16-37). Delft, The Netherlands: Delftse Universitaire Pers.

Tobin, K., & Dawson, G. (1992). Constraints to Curriculum Reform: Teachers and the Myths of Schooling. **Education Technology Research & Development**, 40, 81-92.

Todd, S. (1991). Preparing Tertiary Teachers for Problem-based Learning. In D. Boud & G. Feletti (Eds.), **The Challenge of Problem-based Learning** (pp. 130-136). London: Kogan Place.

Vegt, A.L. van der, & Houtveen, T. (1992). Leraarbegeleiding in soorten en maten [Staff development in various ways]. **Didaktief**, 22 (6), 26-28.

chapter 6

Systematic evaluation of an educational programme as part of the innovation strategy

Marcel Claessens & Wim Jochems

Introduction

The purpose of programme evaluation is to obtain data and to report evaluation results on which decisions about implementation, continuation, modification or termination of a programme can be based. Literature on curriculum innovation puts much emphasis on the integration of an evaluation study as part of the implementation strategy (Romiszowski, 1981). Therefore it was decided to start a systematic evaluation in the context of the implementation of the new curriculum at the faculty of Building Sciences at Delft University of Technology, described in chapters 2 and 3. This contribution provides a brief description of the first stage of that evaluation.

The development of an integral system of programme evaluation was started during the first year of the implementation. In this chapter we will present an evaluation diagram that served as a framework for this study. Next the Delphi procedure will be described which was part of the first stage of the project. Finally, we will provide some results and discuss implications with respect to the implementation of the programme.

An evaluation diagram

Before starting evaluation research one has to realize which model will be appropriate in this particular situation. What evaluation model will be an adequate starting point for this evaluation study? In answering this question it should be noted that the evaluation was asked for by the board and the council of the faculty of Building Sciences. They wanted to be provided with data on the basis of which they would be able to decide how to proceed in implementing PBL in the faculty, for instance where and how to adjust or modify the programme.

In our opinion a decision oriented evaluation model provides an adequate starting point (Popham, 1988). Such a model can be described as "an approach that attempts to increase the relevance of evaluations by taking into account the context and structure of the administrative or political decision-making to which the evaluation results are assumed to contribute." (Scheerens, 1990). In particular Cronbach's viewpoints (1980, 1982) seem relevant. In his view programme evaluation is inherently linked with the political context of a programme. So, in designing an evaluation study not only scientific considerations have to be taken in account, but also the practical and political context are relevant. In his writings he also argues that the evaluator has to serve all the relevant participants in the policy making context. Different groups of participants have different interests, and want answers to specific questions. To overcome the danger of becoming a member of one group, the evaluator has to be a "multi-partisan". So, an evaluation study is likely to become a mixture of studies, rather than a single study.

Another starting point is provided by Scriven (1980). He distinguishes three analytic problems which arise in evaluation. First, the criterion problem has to be solved: what factors have to be taken into account. Second, the measurement problem arises: how will these factors be measured. The last problem is the synthesizing or combinatorial problem: how will the factors be weighted. It will be clear that in a decision oriented evaluation all who participate in the decision making process may have an idea of the factors that have to be weighted. The reason for this is that in this educational setting decision makers, teachers and programme developers are, to a considerable extent, the same faculty members.

Based on these elements an evaluation diagram was developed, the so called bow-tie diagram (see figure 1).

Figure 1: Bow-tie diagram of programme evaluation

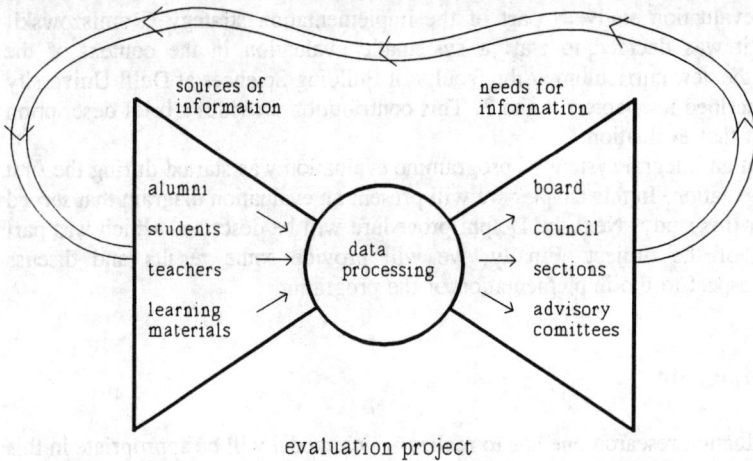

In this diagram, three key aspects can be distinguished (these aspects are in line with Scrivens' analytical problems). First, the evaluator should have a firm understanding of the needs for information. To put this in another way, (s)he has to get an answer to the following question: "Who needs what kind of information?" Several methods can be used to make an inventory of the needs: by interviewing key-informants, through personal communication with participants, or by a more thorough needs assessment survey. As stated before, a decision oriented approach was the most appropriate starting point for this evaluation research. Therefore, the right wing of the butterfly-tie shows the relevant decision making groups at the faculty. Each of these groups will have different opinions on what factors determine the quality of the curriculum. So, it is proper to distinguish these groups. In a PBL-context the role of the individual teacher is decreased. For instance, block groups determine the contents of the programme. In this particular situation it is not appropriate to

50

distinguish teachers as a separate decision making group.

Next, the evaluator has to make an inventory of the sources of information. At this stage, the evaluator looks for all the relevant kinds of evidence evaluation research can obtain. To be more specific, for every need for information, all possible sources of information will be inventoried. Along with these aspects, the evaluator thinks about the ways information can be obtained. In other words, the methods and the instruments of the data gathering will be generated. So, at this stage the evaluator decides on whether to undertake a scientific or a naturalistic evaluation study (or both).

Finally, after the operational stage of the evaluation study (the data gathering), evaluation data are processed and the results will be reported to in a format that is convenient for the audiences. The arrows in the left wing indicate the data the evaluator obtains; the arrows in the right wing point out the reporting of the evaluation results. The arrows at the back of the tie indicate the intended impact of decisions on the sources of information. New results obtained by evaluation research will indicate if, and to what extent these decisions have led to improvements. In this way these arrows emphasize the dynamic nature of the evaluation diagram.

In the diagram the role of the evaluator is that of an intermediary between all the relevant needs and the sources for information. The evaluator operates as a linking agent, because (s)he has an overview of the relevant aspects of the evaluation study. In every evaluation study choices have to be made. By listing all the possible needs for information and sources of information the evaluator will be aware of the choices concerning the kind of research questions, the methods and the instruments that will used, etc.

The Delphi method

According to the diagram, our evaluation study has to start with an understanding of the needs for information. We assessed these needs by means of the Delphi method (Delbecq, Van de Ven & Gustafson, 1975; Linstone & Turoff, 1975). The Delphi method was first used in the nineteen fifties as an instrument to predict future developments. Nowadays it is used as a needs assessment instrument (see Prevoo & Voeten, 1989). In this case, we supposed that faculty members lacked commitment to the programme. In a sense, there were as many viewpoints as faculty members. To put it in another way, it was unclear what elements the evaluation research had to include. A systematic assessment which unravels the nature of dissents was the most appropriate way to collect these viewpoints.

The Delphi method consists of a series of questionnaires. Experts are selected and are asked to respond to successive questionnaires. This way a group meeting is simulated by a paper-and-pencil procedure. This procedure stimulates a process of more rational argumentation. By eliminating face-to-face interaction, the domination of individuals on group decisions is avoided. In general, the procedure is as follows. In the first round, participants are asked to respond to an unstructured, broad question. In the second round, all the responses are transformed into structured items. Participants respond to every item by a written argument and on a Likert scale. In the third round, every participant receives feedback, such as the mean response of all the respondents, and a summary of the written responses (including reasons of disagreement among participants). After reviewing the written responses, participants again respond to the same questionnaire. This process stops when consensus has been reached, or when enough information has been exchanged.

Subjects

Delphi participants are not a random sample of the population, but are a carefully selected group. In this case, most relevant viewpoints on quality had to be included. A list of possible participants was generated through personal communication with experienced faculty members. We asked them to list potential participants. It did not matter whether the candidates these faculty members proposed were for or against the new curriculum; the only criteria for selection were: do they hold a strong opinion on quality and are they appointed for at least two days a week. Hence, we were confident that we would generate a cross-section on the relevant viewpoints among the faculty. In this way a list of 50 potential participants was obtained. To prevent the selection from becoming too subjective the next procedure was applied. The names of these participants were listed in alphabetical order. To each name a number was assigned. With the random numbers procedure, 35 participants were selected.

Procedure

The first questionnaire was examined in a pilot study (5 participants). In February 1992, the first questionnaire was sent to the participants. Participants were asked to respond to the next question: "What aspects do you take into account when you judge the quality of the Building Sciences curriculum?"

The responses were categorized into seven categories, which are presented in figure two.

Figure 2: Categories of educational quality

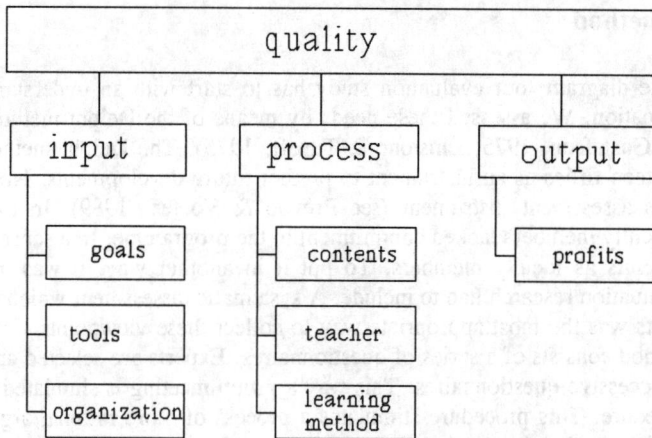

The responses were very different by nature. Some of them were global, for instance "The teacher quality" and some of them were more concrete, for instance "The teacher has to be enthusiastic." Responses which were much the same were grouped together. From each of these groups a single item was constructed that included the quintessence of the responses. Initially, our intention was to ask participants to respond to each item on a five-point Likert-scale and to write an argument for their response. However, in the pilot study it became clear that this "didn't work": the procedure got stuck into vague, global quality statements.

This was a serious threat to the procedure itself and we suspected that continuation in line with the "classical" Delphi method, would generate useless information. So, the procedure was adapted.

Respondents received an overview of the responses from the first questionnaire which included the statements mentioned above, organized into seven categories (see figure 2). Respondents were asked to read the statements, to cross out irrelevant statements, and to add quality statements which had not been included. After this "homework" an interview with the respondents was arranged. The interviews were semi-structured; the categories were used as a guideline. Respondents were asked to name - within each category - the most important standards they use when judging the quality of the Building Sciences curriculum (in concrete terms). From the interviews transcriptions were made and analyzed. The results mentioned below are the main conclusions based on these transcriptions.

Results

The final results are based on 22 interviews, 13 participants did not respond, due of illness, lack of time, etc. In two ways the interviews showed that the following categories were valued as being most important when determining quality: the goals of the curriculum, the content of the curriculum (in relation with the goals of the curriculum) and the teacher quality. First, these categories were emphasized during the interviews (and most of the time during the interviews focused on these categories). Second, at the end of the interviews, respondents were asked to rank the categories (1=most important, 7=least important). These results also show (in terms of mean and median of each category, the times that each categories was given the number 1 and 7) that the above mentioned categories are important. The response to each of these categories will be described more in detail.

The *goals* of the curriculum as a whole are very important. These broad goals reflect viewpoints on Building Sciences as part of society. In a way this is the "mission" of the faculty. To the participants it is crucial that there is some kind of consensus on these viewpoints: without consensus among the faculty the curriculum will be incoherent. Based on these viewpoints the goals of the programme (per graduation, per year, per course) have to be determined.

Building Sciences is an applied science in which analyzing and solving design problems are central issues. The identity of the Building Sciences emerges in fundamental concepts, for instance architectural theories on designing, construction principles, etc. These essential concepts should have an identifiable position in the programme. Students not only have to acquire these concepts but, above all, should also be able to put these concepts into practice (in the so called "design education"). Among the most important skills students have to learn are problem analyzing and solving strategies by reading texts, writing essays, etc., but above all, by being confronted with design problems.

Besides these cognitive aspects (learning and doing), affective goals are crucial: mindless, uncritical students are of little value. So emphasis has to be put on the personal development of students in order to make them creative, innovative and open-minded. This implies for instance a loosely constructed programme (students can choose among a wide range of courses), courses have to be constructed in such a way that students can focus on subjects according to their own abilities and preferences, students have to be stimulated to formulate their own opinion on design problems, etc.

Respondents also considered the contents of the programme to be as an important factor in determining the quality of the curriculum. Participants stressed that the content of the curriculum has to be in line with the goals. Too often, students have to learn things without a clear view on why is it important that these subjects are presented. Basically this has to do with the relevance of the content.

When judging the contents of the programme, respondents also emphasized that the structure has to be logical and clear. In short, the programme, as well as the courses, have to be coherent.

In the professional field of the building sciences a design problem involves many aspects of the building sciences-disciplines. For instance, in designing a railway station not only architectural aspects are crucial, but also knowledge of construction principles and urban design theories. Students have to be prepared for facing such problems. Integration of knowledge and skills from different disciplines is an essential part of the curriculum to many respondents. This means that the programme has to be organized in such a way that the things students have learned can be put into practice in design education. In other words, there has to be a tight link between learning and doing (or theory and practice).

The other important - and to some respondents crucial - factor in determining the quality of the Building Sciences curriculum is the quality of the *faculty staff*. Respondents stressed that the ways in which faculty members are involved in the programme should be in line with their expertise.

This means for instance that architects should not coach students in a block theme which emphasizes managerial aspects of building sciences, or the coaching of students in an urban planning theme by a faculty member whose expertise is in constructions of buildings, etc. In other words, an improvement of the quality of the new programme requires a more careful matching of faculty members expertise with the contents of a specific part of the curriculum. Another aspect of the quality of the faculty staff refers to the effectiveness of teaching, especially in design education. Students differ in their abilities. The individual coaching of the student is crucial with respect to design education. A good teacher must take differences among students into account and coach them according to their abilities. It was also stressed that a teacher should have a firm understanding of the discipline, can motivate students and has be enthusiast for the subject.

Discussion

Quality is a very broad concept. The purpose of the Delphi method was to unravel this concept into more concrete terms. The results show that this aim has not fully been achieved. Quality has been defined in broad terms, but indicators which make these terms more concrete have not been specified.

Although the goals and the contents of the curriculum are considered to be very important in assessing the quality of the programme, it has become clear that respondents share a common vision on building sciences education only to a rather limited degree: design education is crucial, and students have to learn some theoretical (scientific) concepts. But this is a rather abstract, global statement. Disagreement arises when this statement is expressed in concrete terms, for instance the time students have to spend on designing and theory, the extent of a common basic programme (between six months and two years), etc. This can be interpreted in two ways.

First, there is a lack of consensus on essential aspects of the curriculum. There is no broadly shared view on what students have to learn. This may be is a relic of the "old" curriculum. In the "old" curriculum, the design project was the most important instruction principle. This curriculum was very loosely coupled: teachers determined the contents of the project without much faculty supervision. The existence of dissents on crucial aspects of the curriculum is problematic in two ways. The management (board, council) will be hindered in determining a coherent programme which is supported among the faculty. Staff development or other ways of organizational development will be difficult to implement. And there exists an educational problem. Literature on curriculum development stresses that the starting point in developing a programme are clearly stated goals. Without those goals, the programme is likely to be incoherent.

Second, the Delphi method is not a proper procedure for unravelling a broad concept; responding to very concrete statements which are constructed by the researcher, may be more convenient for participants. With respect to the development of an integral system of programme evaluation it is still not clear what factors have to be taken into account and how these factors have to be weighted (cf. Scriven, 1980). Hence, decision makers will be asked to respond to this matter in concrete terms.

With respect to the quality of the faculty staff, it has become clear that teacher plays a crucial part. The teacher is the intermediary between the "arm-chair" curriculum and student learning: (s)he organizes the subject matter attuned to the specific abilities of the students and creates appropriate learning opportunities. In order to be able to play this part well, two requirements have to be met. First, specific expertise is needed whether as a designer or architect, as a manager or planner of building processes, or as a technician who studies out specific technical problems within building sciences. Obviously, it has been assumed wrongly that faculty members can participate in any block, irrespective of the contents of that block. This seems to be an essential distinction between problem-based learning in Medicine as opposed to problem-based learning in Medical Sciences for instance. In the case of Building Sciences faculty members expertise does matter and should be taken into consideration in planning and assigning a course. Second, the programme asks for faculty members who are able to perform different teaching roles: sometimes a lecturer, sometimes a design teacher or a tutor (see also Jochems' contribution in this volume). It has become clear that teacher effectiveness is quite modest and should be increased considerably.

Evaluation studies into this subject are numerous. A few of the methods and instruments for evaluating teacher effectiveness are: student ratings, peer reviews, analysis of learning results of groups of students, and observation of teacher behavior. In the curriculum, many instructional formats are applied: design education, tutor groups, lectures, etc. So it likely to develop instruments adapted to the specific context. For each of these teaching formats specific instruments have to be developed.

References

Cronbach, L.J. (1982). **Designing evaluations of educational and social programs.** San Francisco, California: Jossey-Bass.

Cronbach, L.J. and Associates. (1980). **Toward reform of program evaluation. Aims, methods and institutional arrangements.** San Francisco, California: Jossey-Bass.

Delbecq, A.L., Van de Ven, A.H., & Gustafson, D.H. (1975). **Group techniques for program planning. A guide to nominal group and Delphi processes.** Glenview, Illinois: Scott, Foresman.

Linstone, H.A., & Turoff, M. (eds.). (1975). **The Delphi method: Techniques and applications.** Reading, Massachusetts: Addison-Wesley.

Popham, W.J. (1988). **Educational evaluation** (2nd ed.). Englewood Cliffs, New Jersey: Prentice Hall.

Prevoo, E.G.H.M., & Voeten, M. (1989). **De Delphi-methode voor het bepalen van opleidingsbehoeften** [The Delphi method as a means for assessing training needs]. Gids voor de opleidingspraktijk, 2, 1-19.

Romiszowski, A.J. (1981). **Designing instructional systems: decision making in courseplanning and curriculum design.** London/New York: Kogan Page/Nichols.

Scheerens, J. (1990). Beyond decision-oriented evaluation. In H.J. Walberg & G.E. Haertel (eds.), **The International Encyclopaedia of Educational Evaluation** (pp. 35-40). (Reprinted from: International Journal of Educational Research, 11, no. 1). Oxford: Pergamon Press.

Scriven, M. (1980). **The logic of evaluation.** Inverness, CA: Edgepress.

Worthen, B.R. (1990). Program evaluation. In H.J. Walberg & G.A. Haertel (eds.), **The International Encyclopaedia of Educational Evaluation.** (pp. 42-47). Oxford: Pergamon Press.

56

chapter 7

The assessment of study results in a problem-based curriculum

Pieter Frijns & Erik De Graaff

Introduction

The assessment of learning results is an important aspect of the process of teaching and learning. Students, teachers as well as the community are entitled to information about individual and collective learning achievements. Basically, assessment methods consist of different ways of asking students to demonstrate their knowledge and skills. When assessment results are actually used to decide on the study progress, they have a directing influence on the study behavior of students (Wesdorp et al, 1979; Ebel and Frisbie, 191986). Furthermore, different types of questions evoke different study behavior (Newble & Jaeger, 1983; Frederiksen, 1984). Therefore, the choice of assessment methods should be congruent with the educational and instructional principles of the curriculum.

In this chapter the specific requirements for an evaluation system in a problem-based curriculum are discussed , with the examination system of the Faculty of Building Sciences as an example. The assessment instruments are described as well as the construction procedures. In the last section some empirical findings will be discussed.

Demands of problem-based learning with regard to student assessment

Assessment methods that are used for pass-fail decisions pose demands with respect to the quality of the instruments like sufficient reliability, validity, acceptability, efficiency and effectiveness (Ebel, 1965; Rowntree, 1991). The principles of pbl pose some extra demands on the assessment system to make it congruent to these principles and acceptable for the students.

One of the most important principles of pbl is the responsibility of students for their own learning process and the integration of knowledge and practice (Barrows & Tamblyn, 1980). As a consequence of the emphasis on self-directed learning assessment methods should be selected that do not direct students to a limited domain of study materials. Pbl-students are taught to take responsibility for their own study behavior; choosing their own learning goals and their own learning paths. But, how can we expect them to explore freely all possible sources of information, when they know that the results of their study activities are to be assessed by means of questions on one single book? The most probable outcome of such an assessment strategy is some good old fashioned cramming during the nights before the examination. In order not to frustrate the desired study behavior the assessment system should encompass the whole range of possible learning activities.

A second important feature of pbl with consequences for the choice of assessment methods, is the integration of theory and practice. Within the context of pbl the relevance of knowledge is derived from the application in practical situations. The same principle of relevance for practice constitutes a criterion with respect to the selection of content as well as the choice of format of the assessment methods. A test that focuses on detailed theoretical knowledge, appealing to recognition rather than application of knowledge, rewards the accumulation of isolated facts and may induce students to neglect the aspect of relevance for practice.

A third feature of pbl concerns the integration of disciplines. In a traditional curriculum the teacher is responsible for the content and the assessment of his course. Teachers design their part of the educational programme independent of colleagues who are responsible for other disciplines. A pbl-curriculum, however, is divided into several thematic block periods. Within each block period an integrative educational programme is developed, instead of several monodisciplinary courses programmed parallel. The content of the block is the responsibility of several teachers from various disciplines. As a consequence, the conventional approach to evaluation in which individual teachers or departments are responsible for the assessment of their discipline is not appropriate. The integration of disciplines as well as the integration of knowledge and practice should be incorporated in the evaluation system.

Besides the above mentioned specific demands of pbl Van der Vleuten en Verwijnen (1990) point out some supplementary demands, which are not necessarily related to the educational principles of pbl:

(1)   Assessment should be a continuous process.
(2)   Assessment should serve summative as well as formative purposes.
(3)   The roles of teacher and examiner should be separated as much as possible.

The evaluation system of the Faculty of Building Sciences

The ultimate goal of the Faculty of Building Sciences is to train skilled engineers who are capable to contribute to the development of the science of architecture, as well as the development of the profession. In the old curriculum craftsmanship training consisted a major part. Students spent a lot of time exercising design skills in project work. Next to the design projects students could choose technical skills exercises and lecture courses. The examination programme consisted of a variety of ratings and tests.

As part of the implementation of the new educational programme (see: chapter 2) the Faculty of Building Sciences had to design a new evaluation system, adjusted to the demands of pbl. In the new curriculum design education still constitutes the core of the educational programme. However, one of the main features of the educational innovation was to stimulate the acquisition of knowledge in a thematic block structure, integrating knowledge from different disciplines.

In the new examination system three different competency domains are distinguished: (1) factual knowledge, (2) practical skills and (3) design. For each competency domain specific assessment instruments are developed.

Assessment of knowledge

At the Faculty of Building Sciences knowledge testing takes place at the end of each block period by means of a block test. The content of this paper-and-pencil test reflects the educational goals of the block. Each test consists of 75 to 150 true/false items. In some block tests multiple-choice questions and a few open-ended questions are added. The content of the test is based on a blueprint devised by the block group, specifying the number of questions per discipline and per theme.

The construction of the block test is the responsibility of the coordinator of the block group. The items are written by teachers of the disciplines represented in the block (usually the members of the block group). Before an item is administered in the test, it has to be screened by the Central Test Review Committee, a multidisciplinary group of staff members supported by an educational advisor. The committee criticizes the content, the idiom, and the relevance of the items and suggests alterations. Authors are free to decide how to use the recommendations. Experience shows that according to the committee roughly about 95% of the questions should be altered.

The quality of the test is also checked after the students have completed the test. First, students are invited to comment on the test items. These comments and the psychometric information (e.g. p-value and r_{it}) are discussed within the block group, in presence of the educational advisor of the Central Test Review Committee. Based on this discussion the blockcoordinator may decide to eliminate one or more items.

Technical skills
Technical skills constitute the second competency domain. Within the curriculum of building sciences a broad variety of technical and practical skills are trained. These skills exercises are distributed over the blocks and trained by a number of teachers. The skills-teachers produce ratings for each exercise by means of a number of different instruments. The most frequently employed instruments are:
1 assignments
2 oral presentations
3 written reports/essays
4 work sample

Usually the students have to complete the assignments individually. Sometimes they have to work in couples or a group of students.

Design
Within the curriculum of the Faculty of Building Sciences design education takes a central place. During the six-week blocks students are expected to spend about half of the time working on design assignments. The assignments as well as the criteria for assessment are constructed by the block group. Groups of 15 students are supervised by a teacher, in a studio-like setting. At the end of each block period the results are graded by the teacher.

The reliability of these ratings is a point of serious concern. Raters appear to disagree distinctly about the criteria to be used. For instance, some raters give more attention to the architectonic aspects while others stress the importance of the technical aspects. Some block groups have obliged the teachers to use a second judgement, trying to reduce the subjectivity of the ratings. However, this procedure is not always possible since the grading of design products is very time consuming.

The examination procedure
The examination procedure is designed following the structure of the educational programme. The thematic blocks are regarded as courses, and after each period a final judgement is

given. For each block a partite of judgement is given: (1) a grade for knowledge and (2) a grade for skills. Usually, the grade for knowledge is based on the block test score. The combination of the marks for practical skills and the mark for design constitutes the final grade for skills. The design of these combination rules is the responsibility of the block group. The overall grade for a block is the mean of both grades. A student passes a block when the overall grade for a block is equal or higher than 5.5 on a ten-point-scale.

For the first year of the educational programme, some additional demands are formulated. Students can only pass the first-year examination when the grade for each block is 5.5 or higher as well as the mean over the six first year blocks for both knowledge and skills is higher than 6.0.

Discussion

The examination system of the Faculty of Building Sciences is still in the process of being constructed. Further adjustment to the demands of assessment in a problem-based curriculum entails the development of new instruments within each of the three competence domains as well as revision of the system as a whole.

With respect to the testing of knowledge much energy has been spent on the construction of the block test. The Central Test Review Committee clearly indicates that there are structural problems with the quality of the true-false test items. Partly, this may be caused by a lack of expertise in the construction of this type of questions. It is also suggested, however, that the true-false items tend to focus too much on detailed factual knowledge. As a consequence the intended integration of disciplines is not sustained by the test format. Students are encouraged to integrate knowledge from different disciplines in relation to practice, but they have to account for their learning results on a joined set of monodisciplinairy test items. Both the principles of self-directed learning as well as the integration of discipline knowledge with practice are thus violated. At least, students indicate that the block test frustrates their own responsibility for their learning paths.

One suggestion to overcome this problem is the use of a progress test (Van der Vleuten & Verwijnen, 1990). However, the construction of such a large test, aiming at the end level of the educational programme, is very difficult. Considering the quality problems that already exist with the block test items, this alternative may prove to be unrealistic.

Another solution aims more directly at the type of questions within the system of block tests. It is suggested, that the objectivity of a test does not have to suffer very much when open-ended questions are utilized, despite known disadvantages, like lacking reliability and the time involved with marking (Norman et al, 1991; Van der Vleuten et al, 1991). Open-ended questions are generally more easily to construct than the objective type. It has been shown that the ability to apply knowledge in relation to practice situations can be tested reliably, by means of a case-based short answer type open-ended question (De Graaff et al, 1987; De Graaff, 1989). Recently, it was demonstrated that the marking of such open-ended questions can be improved by a relatively simple structuring of answer models results in an acceptable level of inter-rater reliability (Frijns, 1993).

In the skills domain the distinction between the relatively simple technical basic skills and the complex skill of designing needs to be elaborated. In the area of the basic skills it may be worthwhile to try and develop skills standards (Van Luijk et al, 1986). In this way it can be made clearer to students what is expected from them.

With respect to the more complex skill of designing, the most important problem to overcome is the subjectivity of the ratings. In the marking of design efforts the raters tend to judge against an internalized standard. The design convictions of the rater usually play a crucial part in marking. As a consequence, students spent a lot of time trying to divine which criteria will do the trick with a certain teacher. Research on the process of grading design products at the Faculty of Building Sciences, aims at the development of more structured scoring methods (Frijns, Klerks and De Graaff, in press.).

Following the development of new test methods, a new balance will have to be found between the three competence domains. Since the line between the three domains cannot be drawn sharply (design encompasses both knowledge and basic skills), a multi-trait multi-method design, specifying different instruments and their relative contribution to the respective domains, appears to be more adequate than a straightforward division between domains.

References

Barrows, H.S. & Tamblyn, R.M. (1980). **Problem-based learning: an approach to medical education.** New York: Springer Publishing Company.

Ebel, R.L. (1965). **Measuring educational achievement.** New Jersey: Prentice Hall Inc.

Ebel, R.L. & Frisbie, D.A. (1986). **Essentials of educational measurement.** New Jersey: Prentice Hall Inc.

Fredericksen, N. (1984). **The real test bias: influences of testing on teaching and learning.** American Psychologist, 39, 193-202.

Frijns, P.H.A.M. (1993). **Over structurering van beoordelingsmethoden voor open vragen.** Dissertatie, Maastricht: Rijksuniversiteit Limburg.

Frijns, P., De Graaff, E. & Klerks, M. (in press) **The effect of expertise of raters and structuring of scoring methods on grading in design education.** Conference book of SEFI-conference, 5-7 may 1993.

Newble, D.I., & Jaeger, K. (1983) **The effect of assessment and examinations the learning of medical students.** Medical Education, 17, 165-171.

Norman, G.R., Van der Vleuten, C.P.M. and De Graaff, E. (1991) **Pitfalls in the Pursuit of Objectivity: Issues of Validity, Efficiency and Acceptance.** Medical Education, 25, 119-126.

Rowntree, D. (1991) **Assessing students: How shall we know them?** London: Kogan Page.

Van der Vleuten, C. & Verwijnen, M. (1990). **A system for student assessment** In Van der Vleuten, C., & Wijnen, W. (Eds.) (1990). Problem-based learning: Perspectives from the Maastricht experience. Amsterdam: Thesis.

Van der Vleuten, C.P.M., Norman, G.R. and De Graaff, E. (1991) **Pitfalls in the Pursuit of Objectivity: Issues of Reliability.** Medical Education, 25, 110-118.

Van Luijk, S.J., Van der Vleuten, C.P.M. & Peet, D.G.M. (1986). **The assessment of clinical and technical skills at the Medical School of Maastricht.** In Hart, I.R., Harden, R.M. & Walton, H.J. (Eds.) Newer developments in assessing clinical competence. Montreal: Heal Publ. Ltd., 134-143.

Wesdorp, H.(Ed.) with Blok, H., De Graaff, E., Wolowitsj-Schelvis, A. en Zijlmans, S.(1979) **Studietoetsen en hun effecten op het onderwijs.** SVO-reeks, 15, 's-Gravenhage: Staatsuitgeverij.

Part III

Studies on the Effects of PBL

chapter 8

Instructional techniques and group size

Wim Jochems

Introduction

In Dutch higher education an increasing part of the instruction-time available tends to be spent on lecturing. Even in the case of rather small groups of students, which allow for more fruitful teaching procedures, teachers are inclined to give a lecture. They hardly use classroom-like teaching procedures in which interactions between teacher and students play an important part.

Generally, lectures look like monologues in which a teacher provides the students with information. He or she explains elements of the subject matter to be learned and provides examples and illustrations. In a lecture the students usually are quite passive; they listen to the teacher and they may take notes. Occasionally, the teacher may ask a question to the students. But in general the students are not actively involved in the subject matter; they are 'observing' information instead of processing it (cf. Jackson & Prosser, 1989, p. 55). As a result, teaching and learning become more ore less separated, because learning is postponed until after the lecture, until the night before the next lecture or even until some days before the test. It will be obvious that such a working-method doesn't benefit the productivity of education.

One should realize that in higher education, especially in the first year, lectures are planned because of the large numbers of students. Teachers are confronted with groups of several hundreds of students and it will be clear that they are invited to give lectures. In such circumstances the use of other teaching methods and instructional techniques is very difficult, maybe sometimes even impossible. In order to increase educational productivity, group size and instructional techniques have to be coupled more rationally in planning a curriculum. Therefore group size should depend on the interaction that is required in the process of mastering subject matter. From this point of view a problem-based curriculum is compared with traditional curricula at Delft University of Technology.

In this chapter we first present some data indicating the composition of a problem-based and a traditional curriculum in engineering education. Next educational productivity is considered in relation to group size and instructional techniques. Finally traditional and problem-based curriculum are compared with respect to the degree in which teaching and learning activities are coupled. This leads to some recommendations to improve the problem-based curriculum at the Faculty of Building Sciences at Delft University of Technology.

Problem-based and traditional curriculum in engineering education

In September 1990 the Faculty of Building Sciences started the implementation of a problem-based curriculum. The transition from a traditional to a problem-based curriculum caused some dramatic changes because of a different planning of the curriculum and a different organization of the course. We will limit ourselves to the shift in planning a curriculum and focus on the differences between a traditional and problem-based curriculum in engineering education. Aspects related to teacher behaviors, course materials, testing procedures and so on are left aside in this chapter.

Table 1 presents some data indicating the amount of varying educational methods programmed in a traditional curriculum and a problem-based curriculum, both in engineering education. The data are averages for the first en second year in the Faculty of Building Sciences with a problem-based curriculum and in another seven engineering faculties at Delft University of Technology with traditional curricula. These faculties each have about 300 to 600 students p.a. entering engineering courses.

Table 1: Programmed educational methods in hours per year and hours per week for traditional curricula and a problem-based curriculum in engineering education (averages over first and second year)

curriculum	traditional		problem-based	
	per year	per week	per year	per week
lecture	530	19	110	3
instruction	130	4	430	12
lab work	300	11	250	7
total	960	34	790	22

In traditional curricula these activities are planned in four periods of seven weeks, each period being followed by examination weeks. In this case a curriculum takes 40 weeks a year. A problem-based curriculum has six periods of six weeks each, including the examinations. In addition, both types of curricula have re-examinations at the end of the summer holidays.

As can be seen in Table 1, there are remarkable differences between the problem-based and traditional curriculum with respect to the occurrence of instructional formats. First, the average number of lectures per week is 19 hours in a traditional curriculum versus 3 in a problem-based. In general, these lectures have to be characterized as monologues by a teacher providing explanations and illustrations of the subject matter to large groups of students, on the average several hundreds of students and mounting up to 600 and incidentally even more.

Second, the average amount of instruction is 4 hours per week in a traditional curriculum versus 12 in a problem-based, one third of these being tutorials, also called tutor groups. Instruction refers to a classroom-like situation in which an instructor sets tasks of various kinds to rather small groups of students, providing them with cues, feedback, and so on. Group size varies from about 10 to 40 at the most. The kind of tasks presented to the students depends on the objectives of the instruction, which may be learning to learn, learning to design or learning to master problem solving routines, for instance mathematical ones.

66

Third, in the problem-based curriculum considerably more time is available for self-study. According to the Dutch law on higher education the content of a course should be based on a student workload of 1680 hours a year (see Oort & Pinkster, 1992 for a description of the Dutch engineering education). From this point of view 700 hours p.a. are available for self-study in a traditional curriculum and almost 900 hours p.a. in a problem-based one. Whether these hours are used fruitfully or not, depends of course on the students. But it also depends on the organization of the curriculum and on the teacher. For instance, a course may be organized in such a way that at regular times tests are administered and students' progress is assessed. Or a teacher may stimulate students to work on the subject matter by setting tasks. In other words, there is a difference between both types of curricula with respect to the opportunities for self-study.

In this comparison we don't take lab work into consideration for several reasons. As can be seen in table 1 there isn't a remarkable difference between the two types of curricula with respect to lab work. Besides, lab work in general isn't guided by teachers; these tasks are usually performed by other staff members, for instance by assistant researchers or by technical assistants.

What kind of teaching do these curricula call for? With respect to the teacher, three different roles can be discriminated. One of these roles, of course, is lecturing: the main task of a lecturer is to provide students with information, especially by explaining subject matter. Another role is instructing, which can be described as providing students with opportunities to practice certain skills and procedures, providing them with cues and feedback, and with formal and informal tests in order to assess their progress in mastering the subject matter. A third role is tutoring, which is more or less typical of a problem-based curriculum. It refers to supporting students in learning to learn. It also refers to teaching students how to handle problems in a systematic way, how to formulate adequate learning objectives, how to report orally in a brief and well-structured way and how to stimulating self-study activities (see Wilkerson & Hundert, 1991, pp. 163-167 for a more detailed description).

Educational productivity, group size and instructional techniques

In planning a curriculum one should ask oneself what factors related to teaching methods and learning processes are important for educational productivity. There is quite a lot of evidence that student activity is a crucial factor. According to Guskey's study, 'students' involvement and active participation in instruction are extremely important to learning' ... just as 'providing students with regular and specific feedback' (Guskey, 1988, pp. 25-26). The educational productivity model as presented by Fraser et al. (1987, p. 158 and p. 205) shows that student participation, reinforcement, corrective feedback, and cues are important factors with respect to the method of instruction and the learning process. So in planning a curriculum we should prefer methods of instruction that allow for or, even better, stimulate student activities. To quote Brophy and Alleman (1991, p. 9): 'By "activities" we mean anything that students are expected to do, beyond getting input through reading or listening, in order to learn, practice, apply, evaluate, or in any other way respond to curricular content (content is construed broadly to include knowledge, skills, values, and dispositions to action). Thus, activities may call for *speech* (answer questions or participate in discussion, debate, or role play), *writing* (short answers, longer compositions, research reports), or goal-directed *action* (conduct inquiry, solve problems, construct models or displays). Activities may be done either in or out of the classroom (i.e., as homework); in whole-class, small-group, or individual settings; and under close and continuing teacher supervision or largely independent (on one's own or with peers).' So far Brophy and Alleman.

Assuming these factors to be crucial now the question arises how to use the 'teacher-power' available in a curriculum. Leaving lab work aside for reasons mentioned above, three teaching methods have to be programmed in a curriculum:

* Lectures of course are useful for explaining and illustrating subject matter. This can be done in very large groups of students, e.g. hundreds of students; there is hardly any limitation to group size. Lecturing is quite cheap, but doesn't really produce a lot of learning activities. So in general, the productivity of this instructional format is likely to be rather modest.

* Instructions in a classroomlike setting allow for active student participation with regular and specific feedback. In a classroom with 20 to 40 students the instructor is able to organize learning activities, to control the learning process of each of the students individually and, if necessary, to give cues. He also is able to assess the progress and the results of each of the students. Of course this instructional format is much more expensive, but it can be more productive as compared to lecturing.

* Tutorials are useful if students have to work in close co-operation which requires a lot of interaction between students, e.g. in handling a case. This requires the number of students to be reduced to 10 or 15 in order to enable all the students in a tutor group to participate actively. It will be clear that a tutorial is even more expensive than an instruction, whereas its productivity is probably more or less comparable to that of an instruction.

With respect to planning and organizing a curriculum it is obvious that group size is an important factor. In front of a large group of students a teacher hardly has any choice. A large number of students almost forces him to give a lecture, because other teaching methods and techniques ask for small groups, that is to say groups of about 40 students at the most. So group size and teaching techniques are related in such a way that a restricted group size is a conditio sine qua non for productive teaching. In a large group it is almost impossible for a teacher to create and manage learning activities in a proper way, to give cues and feedback to individual students, to check whether or not a student is or has been working on a task, to assess progress, and so on. That is why teachers are limited to lecturing. As a result the students remain quite passive and the productivity is rather low.

Now at least two implications become clear. First, in planning a curriculum the teaching methods desired should be linked to group size. If student activities are to be supported for one reason or another, small groups are necessary and a tutorial or an instruction has to be planned. In this case a considerable part of the time available should be devoted to providing structured opportunities for students to interact with the content of the course and to provide them with feedback. If the promotion of student activities is rather unimportant, large groups are permitted and a lecture can be planned. In other words, group size determines whether or not it is possible to stimulate and maintain student activity.

Second, there is a need for teachers who are able to develop and to manage student activities in such a way that an efficient learning environment is created (cf. Brophy & Good, 1986, p. 360), not only inside the classroom, but also outside by setting tasks that students have to perform at home. This, in turn, asks for teachers who are able not only to explain subject matter, but also to organize learning activities, to provide cues and feedback, to stimulate students to participate in these activities, to manage small group work and to assess performances.

So in planning a curriculum, the heart of the matter seems to be the management of learning instead of the management of teaching. A curriculum has to be organized in such a way that the student can be actively involved in learning as large a part of the time as possible. This refers to the classroom, but of course also to self-study outside the classroom. In other words, the curriculum should be organized in such a way that student learning, including self-study, can be stimulated and supported maximally by the teacher.

Traditional and problem-based curricula compared

What are the most obvious differences between a traditional and a problem-based curriculum? According to the data in Table 1, the amount of small group work (instructions and tutorials) in a problem-based curriculum is about three times as large as in a traditional curriculum. Therefore, a problem-based curriculum offers more opportunities to activate students and to facilitate student participation. From a theoretical point of view, the problem-based curriculum should be the more productive one. Whether these opportunities are utilized maximally, largely depends on the teachers.

Second, a problem-based curriculum asks for teachers who are able to perform different teacher roles. Depending on whether a lecture, an instruction or a tutorial is programmed, they should be able to use different sets of teaching techniques described in the preceding section. Changing teacher roles has appeared to be very difficult (see chapter 5). Nevertheless, if teachers aren't able to perform all these roles adequately, the assumed benefit of a problem-based curriculum as compared to a traditional one will decrease or even disappear. The difference between both types may be reduced to a difference in group size. By this we mean that in a problem-based curriculum lectures may be given not only in large groups, but also in small groups originally meant for instructions and tutorials. So teacher training is very important in developing a problem-based curriculum, even more important than in traditional curricula.

Third, a problem-based curriculum is more expensive than traditional curricula. Roughly speaking the problem-based curriculum in the Faculty of Building Sciences requires about twice as much 'teacher-time' as compared to the traditional curricula at Delft University of Technology; that is to say, time needed for teaching and the immediate preparation of teaching[1]. On the other hand, in a traditional curriculum testing is considerably more expensive. For instance, the number of regular tests administered in the first year is about 15 in traditional curricula and 6 in a problem-based, leaving retests out of consideration. Besides, the method of testing applied in the problem-based curriculum is less time consuming because of automation. Nevertheless, the Faculty of Building Sciences could reduce costs to some extent by enlarging the number of students in instructions. For instance, the number of participants may be raised to 40 in an instruction and to 15 in a tutorial. If teachers are trained well, they will be able to manage such groups adequately.

Fourth, what about the learning outcomes in a problem-based curriculum? Though some data are available concerning the Faculty of Building Sciences, favoring a problem-based curriculum, it is very difficult to make a fair comparison between student results for the old

---

1 In this respect the difference between the old and the new Building Sciences curriculum is small, because the old curriculum already contained a lot of small group work as compared to the traditional curricula at the Delft University of Technology.

and new curriculum. The transition from a traditional to a problem-based curriculum caused several radical changes complicating a comparison. For instance, course content has been restructured considerably and some subject matter elements have been replaced by others. The method of assessing learning outcomes has been changed radically, too. Besides, the transition to a problem-based curriculum has been used to reconsider the objectives of the course and the standards to be set. Therefore, from a methodological point of view it doesn't make sense to compare the learning outcomes in the old and the new curriculum in a quantitative way.

Recommendations

In order to improve the productivity of the problem-based curriculum at the Faculty of Building Sciences at Delft University of Technology two measures have to be considered. First, the educational activities should be spread over a period of more than 36 weeks, just as in traditional curricula, namely 42 weeks. There are two reasons for this. According to the law a course should be programmed such that a student workload of 1680 hours a year is realized. This is equivalent to a student workload of 40 hours a week during 42 weeks p.a. Another reason is that spreading will enable students to invest a greater amount of time in studying. It should be clear that we don't want to increase the number of lectures, instructions and tutorials nor the time spent on teaching. We just want to increase the time students spend on studying. This might be realized by spreading educational activities over a period of 42 weeks and, at the same time, by setting tasks students have to perform at home in the meanwhile. In this way self-study may be stimulated. Theoretically, the amount of time spent on self-study may increase by 10%. This is likely to produce better learning outcomes.

Second, because teachers only partially utilize the opportunities offered by a problem-based curriculum, more attention has to be given to teacher training and faculty development. This attention should be focused on teachers' abilities to stimulate, support and maintain student participation, to organize and manage student activities and to give cues and feedback to individual students. If teachers don't master these techniques, the opportunities offered by a problem-based curriculum will get lost more or less. In this case, the higher costs of a problem-based curriculum will certainly not be compensated for by better learning outcomes. That is why teacher training is so important in a problem-based curriculum.

References

Brophy, J. & Alleman, J. (1991). Activities as instructional tools: a framework for analysis and evaluation. **Educational Researcher**, 20, 4, 9-23.

Brophy, J. & Good, Th.L. (1986). Teacher behavior and student achievement. In M.C. Wittrock (Ed.). **Handbook of research on teaching** (pp. 328-375). New York: Macmillan Publ. Comp.

Fraser, B.J., Walberg, H.J., Welch, W.W. & Hattie, J.A. (1987). Syntheses of educational productivity research. **International Journal of Educational Research**, 11, 2, 145-252.

Guskey, T.R. (1988). **Improving student learning in college classrooms.** Springfield, Ill.: Charles

C. Thomas Publ.

Jackson, M.W. & Prosser, M.T. (1989). Less lecturing, more learning. **Studies in Higher Education**, 14, 1, 55-68.

Oort, H.J. van & Pinkster, J. (1992). The Netherlands engineering education: within the framework of the Dutch educational system. **European Journal of Engineering Education**, 17, 1, 9-16.

Wilkerson L.A. & Hundert, E.M. (1991). Becoming a problem-based tutor: increasing self-awareness through faculty development. In D. Boud G. Feletti (Eds.). **The challenge of problem-based learning** (pp. 159-171). London: Kogan Page.

chapter 9

Directing learning activities by different types of tasks

Kees van Wijngaarden & Jos Willems

Introduction

The Problem-Based Learning (PBL) curriculum of the Faculty of Policy and Administrative Studies (FPAS) utilises problems and other types of tasks as the starting-point for student learning activities. Students determine their own learning goals and choose which learning activities they will perform (Schmidt, 1982). Since education can be assumed to be a goal directed activity, the intention is to guide student learning activities. A teacher can achieve this goal by lecturing or by means of different kinds of assignments. In the latter case the relationship is as follows:

Instruction (Tasks) →→→ Learning activities →→→ Learning achievements

To find out about the directing effects of tasks it is necessary to study the learning activities (Dolmans, Gijselaers en Schmidt, 1991).
The FPAS-curriculum includes several types of tasks which are defined as: problem tasks, application tasks and study tasks. It is generally expected that different kinds of tasks will result in different types of learning activities. Whether the different types of tasks do result in the expected learning activities has yet to be established. A task contains several elements that are intended to direct a student towards the expected learning activities. Tasks differ in the degree to which directing elements are present. The relative contribution of these elements needs to be investigated.
To improve understanding of the effects of PBL tasks in directing elements of the students learning activities, two related research studies were performed. The first study was a survey in which we examined the learning activities associated with the different types of tasks and assessed the extent to which the directing elements contribute to different learning activities. The second study was related to the first. We adapted some tasks by including more directing elements and we have looked for different types of learning activities in both the adapted and unadapted tasks.

Survey of tasks

The first exploratory study was focused on two questions.
* Do students undertake different learning activities when performing different tasks?
* To what extent do different elements of tasks have a guiding effect on learning activities?
For this preliminary study it was necessary to consider the purpose and objectives of the

tasks, the learning activities involved and the directing elements in the task.

Objective of the tasks

The curriculum includes several types of tasks: problem tasks, study tasks and application tasks. Each type of task has a different purpose and has different objectives (Moust, Bouhuijs & Schmidt, 1983):

Problem task: Students are given a problem and have to make their own learning objectives and problem definition. They must find the literature to attain to the learning objectives and to find a solution for the problem.

Study tasks: Students have to study the relevant literature. Sometimes they have to make schemes and summaries.

Application task: Students must use their existing knowledge in new or different circumstances. Students must apply their previously acquired knowledge to the problem at hand.

Learning activities

The categories of learning activities are based on the Inventory Learning Processes (ILP) of Schmeck (1983) which are based on the depth of processing:

Deep processing: This is process of verbal classification of information and comparison.

Elaborate processing: This involves seeking concrete associations or examples which permit the student to interpret the facts learned.

Fact Retention: This is the way people carefully process (and thus store) new information regardless of what other information processing strategies they might employ.

Structuring: The making of schemes and summaries.

By incorporating combinations of these learning activities in the tasks it should be possible to produce the desired learning activities. A problem task is intended to lead to deep processing and some degree of elaborate processing. An application task should demand elaborate processing, some deep processing and fact retention. A study task should lead to fact retention and structuring by the students. These are the expected learning activities which would be produced by the different types of tasks.

Directing elements

Tasks incorporate various kinds of directing elements which guide the students during the execution of a task (Koper, 1989 and Wolters & Willems, 1984). The following directing elements can be used:

Introduction: explanation of the context of the task.

Type of the task: name of the task.

Learning goals: directing the student to what must be known when the task has been completed.

Task goals: form in which the knowledge should be presented.

Specific instruction: working procedure to be used.

Reference information: information/knowledge essential to the completion of the task

Relevant literature: literature the students must study to accomplish the task.

Assignment: instruction in which the problem is summarised in the form of a question the students must answer.

Methods

Subjects and procedure
In this study 120 students volunteered as subjects. They were divided into 10 PBL-groups, with two groups to each tutor. When the students had completed a task they were given a questionnaire about their learning activities while performing the task.

Instruments
This study is based on the interpretation of the tasks and the results of a questionnaire. The tasks formed part of the second block of the curriculum that is offered in the first year of the FPAS in Nijmegen. Nine tasks were involved: 3 problem tasks, 3 study tasks and 3 application tasks.

Table 1: Task type and directing elements

	Problem task	Application task	Study task
Introduction	--	--	--
Type of task	++	++	++
Learning goal	--	--	--
Task goal	--	++	++
Specific instruction	++	++	++
Reference information	--	++	--
Relevant literature	--	--	++
Assignment	--	--	++

The questionnaire was based on the Inventory Learning Processes (ILP) (Schmeck et al.., 1983) and called Actual Learning Activities (ALA).

Variables
There were two independent variables in study 1: type of tasks and directing elements. The dependent variables were the actual learning activities of the students.

Results
A principle component analysis of the questionnaire resulted in two stable factors: Deep processing ($\alpha = .64$) and Structuring ($\alpha = .62$). These factors accounted for $\pm 55\%$ of the variance.

Table 2: Difference in degree of deep processing produced by different types of tasks

	Application task	Study task
Problem task	t = -3.47**	t = -3.73**
Application task		t = .13

** $\alpha = 0.01$

The first question considered was whether the learning activities differ for each type of task.

A t-test for paired examinations is used to examine the difference between the types of task. For example, on the factor deep processing, the application task (t = 3.73) and the study task (t = 3.47) both score higher then the problem task (See table 2).

It appeared that problem tasks (t = 4.65) and study tasks (t = 4.50) (See table 3) gave rise to more structuring than application tasks.

Table 3: Difference in degree of structuring produced by different types of tasks

	Application task	Study task
Problem task	t = 4.65**	t = 1.36
Application task		t = -4.51**

** α = 0.01

The second question posed concerned the effect of the directing elements on the learning activities. The results are shown in table 4. The most interesting result is that the absence of a task goal, mentioning of relevant literature and an assignment, leads to more structuring. The absence of these elements may be the reason why students resort to increased structuring. Schmeck (1983) indicates that students may fall back on methodical study when they do not know how to process the subject matter. So the absence of structuring is an indication that the students have employed more deep processing activities.

Table 4: Effect of the directing elements on the factors deep processing and structuring

	Deep processing		Structuring	
	Mean	t-value	Mean	t-value
Introduction				
absent	12.22	4.04**	7.33	1.03
present	11.47		7.53	
Task goal				
absent	11.90	-1.56	7.97	7.71**
present	12.19		6.87	
Reference information				
absent	12.14	1.16	7.34	1.16
present	11.64		7.55	
Relevant literature				
absent	11.67	-7.	7.64	2.93**
present	12.49	96**	7.08	
Assignment				
absent	12.68	1.45	9.04	13.09**
present	12.28		6.76	
Type of task				
absent	12.32	1.19	6.71	-3.79**
present	11.85		8.96	

** α = 0.01

Conclusion from the survey of tasks

One conclusion is that, especially in problem tasks, we do not find the expected learning activities. We expected that the students will engage in deep processing activities but we found more structuring and less deep processing than anticipated. A possible explanation is that students postpone the deep processing activities until they are required to write an essay at a later date. Last activities were not examined in this study. If this is true the students engaged in two separate types of activities. The first was the searching for information and literature. The second activities were the deep processing activities. This is contrary to the intention of Problem Based Learning, where deep processing activities are supposed to take place during the search for and studying the literature relevant for the solution of the problem (See Table 5).

Table 5: Comparison between the expected learning activities (ELA) and the actual learning activities (ALA)

	Problem task		Study task		Application task	
	ELA	ALA	ELA	ALA	ELA	ALA
Deep processing	+/-	--	--	++	++	++
Structuring	--	++	++	++	--	--

The absence of a task goal and an assignment leads to more structuring and if a student does more structuring he will have less time for deep processing activities. In other words the absence of guidance in a task will lead to less deep processing. A problem task provides less guidance than other types of task. In the 2.4 we found less deep processing activities than anticipated. The absence of guidance in the problem tasks may provide another explanation for increased structuring in a problem task.
In study 2 we examined whether more guidance in a problem task would lead to more deep processing activities by the students. This guidance consists of a well-described task goal and an assignment on how to carry out these tasks.

Directing elements in problem tasks

Study 2 is an experimental study using a group with standard task conditions as a control group and another group with adapted tasks. We are searching for an answer to the following questions with regard to the two groups:
* Is there a difference between intended and actual learning activities?
The intended learning activities are the activities that the student expected to perform and the actual learning activities are those done by the student while performing the task.
* What is the influence of the learning style, tasks and intended learning activities on the actual learning activities?

Methods

Subjects and procedure
In this study 130 students were involved. There were 10 PBL-groups with 5 tutors, each with two PBL-groups. In the first session all the PBL-groups were given the learning style questionnaire. After this five groups were given the standard task and five groups got the adapted tasks. Before each task every student had to state the way he intended to perform the task (Intended Learning Activities). After performing the task the students were asked to complete an ALA questionnaire.

Instruments
In this study in order to ensure that students incorporated deep processing in their activities, the problem tasks were adapted to include more guidance. In this way less structuring was needed and as supposed more deep processing possible. This guidance consisted of a clearly defined specific instruction and an assignment. The task goal is stated in the specific instruction. In the adapted tasks the following directing elements were present (see figure 1):
* Type of task
* Assignment
* Specific instruction

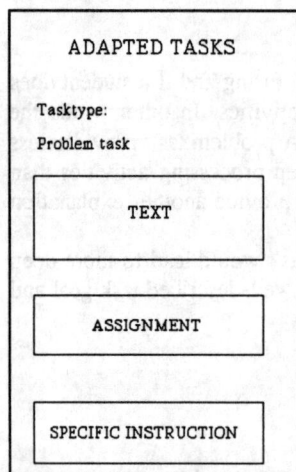

Figure 1: Adapted tasks   Figure 2: Standard tasks

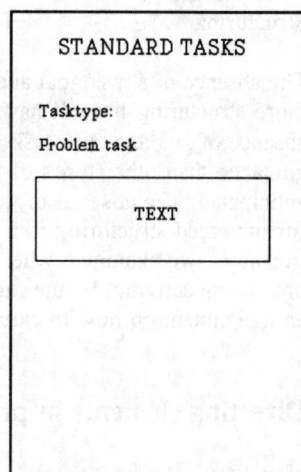

The same text was used for both the standard and the adapted tasks. In both cases the learning objective was the same. In the assignment the students were given a clearly defined problem/question to answer or solve. This was related to the text. The specific instruction was intended to guide the students to the expected learning activities. The student was told what must be done when performing the task.

The first questionnaire was intended to assess the student's learning styles. It is a condensed version of the questionnaire: Inventory of Learning Styles of Vermunt, 1991. The second was used to measure the intended learning activities, i.e. the activities the student intended to do.

The third questionnaire assessed the actual learning activities. The last two questionnaires are based on the Inventory Learning Processes (ILP) of Schmeck, 1983.

Variables
The independent variables were the standard tasks and the adapted tasks. The dependent variables were the intended learning activities and the actual learning activities. The learning style was a control variable.

Results
The results of the principal component analysis of the intended and actual learning activities were given below. The intended learning activities incorporated two stable factors: Deep processing ($\alpha = .62$) and Fact Retention + Structuring ($\alpha = .52$). These factors accounted for 37% of the variance.

A principle component analysis of the adapted actual learning activities resulted in three stable factors: Deep processing ($\alpha = .73$ Structuring ($\alpha = .76$) Fact Retention ($\alpha = .61$). These three factors accounted for 57% of the variance.

The difference between the standard and adapted tasks was evaluated by using a t-test for unpaired groups. No differences were found between the intended and actual learning activities No significant difference was found between the two tasks as can be seen from the t-values (See table 6).

Table 6: Difference between effects of the Standard and the Adapted Tasks on the Intended and Actual Learning Activities

| | Adapted Tasks | | Standard Tasks | | |
	Mean	St.dev.	Mean	St.dev.	t-value
Intended Learning Activities					
Deep processing	60.66	9.33	61.86	9.71	-.10
Fact Retention + Structuring	41.81	8.54	40.92	9.05	.49
Actual Learning Activities					
Deep processing	10.91	44.80	43.81	9.70	.44
Fact Retention	11.41	3.82	10.62	3.90	.96
Structuring	29.30	8.95	27.98	9.89	.65

The influence of the different variables on the actual learning activities was evaluated by using a multi variate variance analysis (Manova) (See table 7).

The intended learning activities have an effect on the actual learning activities. When a student has intended to employ deep processing activities he usually does deep processing activities (task 9: $\beta = .55$ and task 11: $\beta = .42$). If the student has intended to ensure fact retention and structuring he usually achieves this (task 9: $\beta = .59$). For tasks 6 and 11 there were no direct effect but there were interaction effects with the learning styles and the tasks. In task 6 there was interaction between the intended learning activities (deep processing and fact retention + structuring), tasks and learning styles (interaction effect 1: $F = 2.39$ and interaction effect 2: $F = 2.62$). Only in task 11 there was interaction between fact retention and structuring and the tasks (interaction effect 3: $F = 4.69$).

Table 7: Influence of the Tasks, the three Typical Learning Styles and the Intended Learning Activities on the Actual Learning Activities

	Multi-variate	Univariate Deep processing		Fact Retention		Structuring	
	F	β	F	β	F	β	F
Task 6							
Interaction effect 1	2.39**		2.18		3.02*		2.79*
Interaction effect 2	2.62**		1.77		2.79*		3.65*
Task 9							
Intended learn.act.	2.07*	.55*		.07		.27	
Deep processing		.36		.07		.59**	
Fact ret. + Structuring	.42		1.18		.22		.33
Learning styles	.28		.05		.02		.76
Task 11							
Deep processing	2.20*	.42**		.01		.17	
Interaction effect 3	4.69**		.21		7.19**		8.17**
Learning styles	1.21		2.75	.72			1.91

** $\alpha < 0{,}01$ * $\alpha < 0{,}05$

Conclusions

The main conclusion is that using adapted tasks does not ensure that deep processing will be incorporated into the students learning activities. We have found no difference between the results produced by the adapted and standard tasks.

We tried to improve this learning situation by increased guidance in the tasks. The guidance involved incorporating more directing elements in a task, however these directing elements were not strong enough to change the students learning activities. Apparently in order to change their learning activities the students need more or different guidance which, for example, may be generated by the group process. In these two studies we have devoted little attention to the group process. The purposed of using problem based learning is that students should discuss the tasks and the results in small groups. They can then guide each other. A mentor is also present in these small groups. His task is to control the group processes that take place. The guiding role of the students and the mentor is has not yet been studied in detail.

The two studies described were devoted to research on learning activities but they did not reveal why students used the activities in question or why they used particular activities at specific times. More research is necessary to provide more insight into what the students have in mind while searching for and studying the relevant literature: is it to solve the problem or just the need to acquire whatever information is in the book.

Two subjects for further research remain: first the directing effects of the group process on the learning activities of students, bearing in mind that the directing elements are not strong enough to guide the students. Additional guidance may be found in the group process which is not yet understood. Secondly the question: "what guides/motivates a student when he is searching for literature while performing the task?" The answer to this question should provide insight into what a student is thinking when executing the task.

References

Dolmans, D.H.J.M., Gijselaers, W.H. & Schmidt, H.G. (1991). Kunnen toetsen meten wat studenten weten. In: J.K. Koppen, H. Stroomberg & M.van der Kamp. **Hoger onderwijs en Volwasseneducatie.** Amsterdam.

Koper, E.J.R. (1989). **Leertaken onder de loep.** Heerlen.

Moust, J.H.C., Bouhuijs, P.A.J.& Schmidt, H.G.(1989). **Probleemgestuurd leren, een wegwijzer voor studenten.** Groningen: Wolters-Noordhoff.

Schmeck, R.R. (1983). Learning Style of College Students. In: Dillon, R.F. & Schmeck, R.R. **Individual differences in cognition,** 1. 233-274, New York.

Schmidt, H.G. (1982). **Activatie van voorkennis, intrinsieke motivatie en de verwerking van tekst.** Apeldoorn: Van Walraven.

Vermunt, J.D.H.M. (1991). Leerstrategieën van studenten in een zelfinstructie leeromgeving. **Pedagogische Studiën.** 7, 315-323.

Willems, J.M.H.M. (1987). **Studietaken als instructiemiddel.** Nijmegen: Academisch proefschrift.

Wolters, L.A.M.M. & Willems, J.M.H.M. (1984). **Studietaken: bedenken en vormgeven van opdrachten voor uw onderwijs.** Nijmegen: Internal publication IOWO.

chapter 10

University students' descriptions of their experience of tutorial groups

Charles Anderson

Background

Tutorials, small group discussions which focus on some aspect of an academic discipline and which are customarily lead by a lecturer, still form an integral part of the teaching which undergraduate students receive in UK institutions of higher education. These tutorials usually take place every week during term time in each of a students courses and may take a number of different forms. Some center around either a wide-ranging, or very focused, discussion of a particular topic. In others an individual student, or a subgroup of students within the tutorial may make a short presentation which is followed by wider discussion. In science based subjects and also in some social science subjects, discussion usually centers around the solution of problems and the wider points of theory that are raised by particular problems. Particularly in the first year of undergraduate study, tutorials may also serve as a forum for passing on advice concerning essay writing and other academic tasks.

Turning to past academic research on tutorials, there was an upsurge of interest in studying tutorials in the period of the late 1960's and 1970's. There have been fewer studies conducted in more recent years. Much of the work conducted on tutorials has been concerned with identifying the conditions which facilitate a good flow of high quality discussion in small groups; and there have been many action research based projects which have evaluated somewhat innovative approaches to small group discussion in higher education(Jaques, 1992). The principal theoretical basis of much of the research has been the literature on group dynamics and it has also been informed to some extent by work on therapeutic groups. The accent in most studies has been on looking at processes in small groups rather than at content.

This chapter presents some of the findings of a fairly large study that was conducted in the academic year 1991 to 1992 of tutorials in the Faculty of Social Sciences at the University of Edinburgh. This study was prompted by two main sources of personal interest in small group teaching One source is a concern with policy and practice. The wider context of the higher education system in the UK has changed very considerably from the period of the 1970's when much research was conducted on tutorials. In recent years there has been a considerable expansion in student numbers in British universities without any corresponding increase in staff numbers. This has in many cases led to a rise in the size of tutorial groups, and some large departments in my own university have moved from weekly tutorials for first year undergraduates to fortnightly tutorials. Tutorials as a form of teaching are therefore under some pressure, and it seemed timely to conduct a study of them during this period of considerable change in the higher education system in the UK. The other strong source of personal interest in this area came from a desire to investigate features of discourse in academic settings and how these features might be influenced by the purposes of the participants. Future publications will focus on the analysis of aspects of the content and forms of the talk which was recorded in tutorials. The present chapter, however, has as its focus not theorizing about talk itself but students' descriptions of their experience of tutorial groups and issues which these descriptions raise for practice.

Problem-based learning and the negotiation of understanding

Before giving a summary account of students' perceptions of their experience of tutorial groups, it is appropriate to highlight the links between the study which is presented in this chapter and the general theme of problem-based learning. Many problem-based courses in higher education aim not only to assist students to reach well reasoned solutions but also to encourage them to be able to communicate these solutions clearly in speech and writing. For example, in describing his aims in devising a problem-based module in mechanical engineering, Cawley writes about how he "decided to convert the course to a problem-based format and to broaden the original aim of merely transmitting technical content to include developing the professional skills of using this material to solve real problems, and of communicating the solutions effectively"(Cawley,1991). Effective problem solving group work also requires the skills of both vigorously debating, negotiating, solutions and acting in a cooperative manner with others. Given this concern with enhancing communication skills, students' accounts of what makes for an effective small group discussion may be of some value to academics who are designing problem-based courses.

Method

Methods used in the study as a whole

The present study looked at a number of tutorials conducted by each of ten tutors, from a range of very different disciplines within the Faculty of Social Sciences (see Table 1.), and covering all the four years of undergraduate teaching. The principal methods of investigation were:
* non-participant observation of the tutorials themselves,
* interviews with the tutors concerning their aims for, beliefs and feelings about tutorials,
* interviews with a sample of the students who took part in the tutorials which were observed.

A key consideration in sampling was the wish to observe 'good practice' in the conduct of tutorials. The ten lecturers whose tutorials were observed had a reputation among colleagues and students as being skilled in facilitating small group discussion.

Table 1

Tutor 1	Tutor 2	Tutor 3	Tutor 4	Tutor 5
Psychology	Psychology	Sociology	Economic & Social History	Economic & Social History
1st & 4th year group	1st & 4th year group	2nd year group	1st[*] & 2nd year group	1st[*] & 1st year group

Tutor 6	Tutor 7	Tutor 8	Tutor 9	Tutor 10
Economic & Social History	Nursing Studies	Nursing Studies	Accountancy	Psychology statistics
3rd year group	3rd year group	3rd & 4th year group	3rd year group	1st year group

* The same starred 1st year group was observed led by both Tutor 4 and Tutor 5

Features of the sample and the nature of the interviews conducted with students
The findings which are reported in this chapter come from interviews which were conducted with 52 students drawn from the groups led by tutors 1 to 9 described in Table 1. The fact that I had observed the tutorial groups in which the students had participated over a period of weeks, meant that when I came to interview students I had a reasonably clear sense of their individual patterns of participation in tutorials to compare with their own perceptions of their aims and performance in tutorials. It is recognized that caution needs to be exercised in generalizing from the findings of this present study. Students in other UK institutions may have somewhat different experiences of tutorials and science students may not altogether share the experience and perceptions of tutorials of social science students.
One important background detail which needs to be mentioned is that in Scottish universities a first degree with honors is taken over the period of four years and in each of the first two years of the degree students take three different subjects. So by the time they reach third or fourth year they have quite a wide experience of tutorials in different subjects and of the differing personal styles of tutors. All of the interviews were conducted by the author. Most of the interviews lasted between thirty-five to forty minutes, although there were quite a few which were over an hour in length. Some of the first year students whom I interviewed, not surprisingly given that they had less experience to comment on, gave much shorter responses, and their interviews were just under thirty minutes in length.
The style of the interviews was interactive and focused. As an interviewer I faced the task of balancing the desire to give students freedom to construct their own accounts of what was salient for them in tutorials against my wish as a researcher to gain information on specific aspects of tutorials and to gain broadly comparable data across subjects. The balance was struck more in my own favor, but I did try to ensure that the interviews did contain very general prompts which allowed the students to have some control and tell their own story in their own terms; and where students were giving an account of areas which were not on my own list of topics to investigate they were encouraged to proceed. I indicated at the beginning of each interview that there were specific aspects of tutorials that I would like to hear their thoughts on, but that if they themselves did not consider that these questions made sense to them, or were irrelevant to them, they should say so very clearly. I also stated in each interview that if a student felt that I had posed a question which seemed too general in its

form, that he or she should make it much more specific in ways which seemed appropriate to him or her.

In asking initial questions about an aspect of tutorials I attempted to cast the questions in a very open-ended form which would not constrain the students answer. Once students did respond to an initial question, however, I took a more active role and often made requests for clarification and for expansion. To reduce problems at the stage of the interpretation of the data, I quite frequently presented students with my reading of what they had just been saying for comment. Most of the aspects of tutorials on which I attempted to collect data from informants are summarized in Table 2.

The analysis of interview material

All of the interviews were fully transcribed and then a very time-consuming process of reading and re-reading the transcripts in a cyclical manner was undertaken to provide a rigorous qualitative analysis of the data. Statements about particular aspects of tutorials, or common themes in the students' accounts, were noted, coded and collected together in separate computer data files. Any salient differences between students in reactions to, thoughts about, particular aspects of tutorials were identified and possible reasons for the differences were then explored. Individual interviews were analyzed to see whether dominant themes emerged in the way that each individual viewed tutorials. It was recognized that students' reactions to, constructions of, particular aspects of tutorials need to be interpreted in the context of their interview as a whole. In conducting the analysis I was also on the look-out for variability, as well as consistency, in the accounts that individual students gave of particular aspects of tutorials.

Table 2: Main topics explored in the interviews with students

* inviting comments
* likes /dislikes
* what helps, what hinders their personal participation
* formal or informal atmosphere in the group, and how that affects learning
* reactions to other students' contributions
* reactions to tutors' direct questions and to tutors' 'clarifying' questions
* connections with other parts of the course, in particular the lectures
* sufficient opportunity in tutorials to explore personal problems in understanding course content?
* what makes it easy or difficult to listen actively in tutorials
* willingness to debate a point with another student
* preference for more focused or for more wide-ranging discussion
* questions concerning tutorials where students themselves are asked to present a short paper
* quantity and quality of advice given in tutorials on reading, essay-writing, exam preparation
* exploring whether tutorials have any social benefits
* preferred size of tutorial group

Findings

Features identified as important for active debate and listening

In this brief chapter it is not possible to present a fine-grained analysis of the rich accounts which the students provided of their experience. The strategy for reporting results is to give a very summary account of the features which were identified as important for active debate and listening by most of the informants. A slightly more detailed account will then be provided of a number of topics concerning tutorials which may also have relevance for problem-based learning groups. Table 3 lists, in no particular rank order, what the students saw as key features in promoting active participation and listening in a tutorial.

Table 3: Features identified by students as important for promoting active participation and listening

* skills of the tutor in facilitating debate in an engaged manner
* informal group atmosphere
* students themselves investing effort in discussion and the creation of a good group atmosphere
* self-esteem, confidence
* not too large a tutorial group
* personal interest in the particular subject matter being discussed
* the nature of the subject matter being discussed
* personal knowledge of the topic under debate and general background of knowledge of the discipline
* appropriate preparation
* not too much pressure from other coursework
* clear focus for preparation provided by the tutor

The features listed in the top half of Table 3 which are concerned with aspects of tutor style and group dynamics have also been clearly identified as important in earlier research on tutorials (Brown and Atkins, 1988, Chp.4). Students in the present study identified interest, enthusiasm on the part of the tutor him or herself as strongly influencing their participation. A number of respondents drew a sharp contrast between tutors whom they regarded as unsatisfactory who were merely routinely going through the motions of their job, as opposed to those who displayed real interest, enthusiasm and engagement with their students. There was a general expectation that tutors would energetically apply the skills appropriate for facilitating debate. The following quotes from a third year male Accountancy student give some sense of the expectations that students expressed for the tutor to exercise an active facilitating role; and they suggest some reasons why tutors may often not be free to adopt a more 'hands-off' style of facilitation. S1 *"I think the tutor has got to make an attempt to try and bring in everybody. I think [Tutor X] is very good at that - because he does try to get everybody to say at least something during the tutorial which some others don't do. Which is, you know, you get three people who dominate the discussion all the time and then the others just sit by, you know, sit on the sidelines and that's not a good thing."* S1 *"I think it is necessary for them to ask questions if the group's silent but if - if possible - I think the best tutorial is when the interactions are between the students actually and that helps."* Interviewer *"Do you find that happens much?"* S1 *"Ehm. Not really. No. No, I think that's*

why there is the definite need for the tutor to chip in there, now and again. "
Other aspects identified by many of the respondents as affecting the quantity and quality of participation were:
* an informal group atmosphere, students themselves being prepared to invest effort in the discussion
* the creation of a good atmosphere and within-individual factors such as self-esteem and confidence.

The size of the tutorial was also seen as an important matter in determining willingness to take part; and the two following extracts illustrate the ways in which the effects of tutorial size were described. The first quote is from a third year, male Accountancy student: S2 *"[You] feel yourself just, you know, almost in a lecture scenario again where you're just one of a larger group whereas if you've five, six, seven, you know, you're more fundamental you're needed, you have to keep on the ball, keep yourself going, yeah. "* Here is a third year woman student on an Economic and Social History course giving her thoughts on group size and its effects on her participation: S3 *"I think groups should be about eight people maybe. I don't think any more than that because I've had some groups where you've got thirteen, twelve, thirteen people. If that's the case then honestly I tend to think well it's not my turn, I'll let so and so speak, or whatever. So I think if there are about six to eight people then it's a lot easier - it's a lot less formal I think a lot of the time. "*

The remaining features listed in Table 3 are related in some way or other to the content of discussion and emerge very clearly in the present study as matters which students perceive to be important in facilitating participation in, and engaged reflection on, the discussion. These features have attracted less attention in previous studies. *Personal interest,* or lack of interest, in an individual topic within the curriculum of a course was seen by most students as a very important matter in determining how they participated and listened. Quite a number of students also indicated that they saw some subject areas, even within a particular discipline, as much more amenable to active debate than others. *Personal knowledge* of the topic under debate featured strongly in the account which most students gave of the factors which influenced their participation in discussion.

The students described the importance of preparation, in terms of reading relevant literature or gaining familiarity in solving a particular class of problem, to ensure that they would come along to a tutorial armed with the requisite personal knowledge. Disapproval was expressed of peers who came along to tutorials unprepared and therefore unable to make an appropriate contribution. However, the preparation that could be achieved was constrained by the competing demands of other coursework , such as essays, that had to be completed: and given that this other work was very often formally assessed, whereas tutorial work is not, it tended to take precedence. Preparing effectively for tutorials was also regarded by some students as a matter which depended not only on their own investment of time and effort, but also on the actions of the tutors. Preparation was seen as easier to achieve when tutors provided well focused reading and a clearly defined topic for the next tutorial.

Staying on the theme of how students themselves saw the subject knowledge that they possessed affecting both the quantity and quality of their input to the discussion, a number of third and fourth year students commented on how the nature of discussion in tutorials had changed as they progressed through the years and gained more knowledge in a particular discipline. Here, for example, is one fourth year student talking first of all about the problems which can arise when first year students are not given sufficiently focused advice on preparing for a tutorial and do not have background knowledge of the subject on which they can draw. S4 *"I dislike tutorials where we haven't been - I mean it happened a lot in first year, we weren't told right prepare something -- and I suppose in any given area, particularly in first year if you're not given any kind of instructions to go and do some reading beforehand, then people have much the same view, you know like the sort of layman's view of the subject, and there's no discussion at all."* The same student then went on to draw a contrast between first and later years of study: *"--- it's more difficult in the lower years - I mean a lot of the stuff in the higher years, the discussion arises from people's own views anyway that they've acquired through the years. There's a lot more general knowledge obviously in the subjects that you've picked up."*

The effects of the wider context of schooling

Although most students commented on how immediately obvious aspects of their learning environment such as other work and aspects of course organization influenced their experience of tutorials, only a few reflected on the influence that wider features of the education system had on their performance in group work. These few students commented on how the individualistic, competitive ethos of the schooling that many individuals had received prior to entering university meant that it was difficult for them to make the transition to a "less selfish", more cooperative form of group work. Here are two quotes on this theme. The first is from a third year student who herself was very willing to debate and share ideas generously: S5 *"I mean the way that we are taught at schools is such an individualistic way that I think it is really difficult to overcome that: and we were taught sort of when you write, you know you write like that [gesture of covering up work] and then to go into a tutorial when you're actually sharing your ideas, I mean people are very, very selfish. I mean I know people that say well no, because there is a limit to how many views you can give -- I mean people do still think like that."*

A male mature third year student contrasted his experience of work groups with groups at university: S6 *"On your own, you don't cooperate at the school: and that's a barrier to cooperating --. Whereas if you've worked before, you do cooperate just with the nature of work processes involved I think, so you're used to it. You don't feel so threatened just to ask somebody ---."*

These quotes highlight the adjustments in perspectives and behavior that students may need to make in coming to group work and the need to provide very clear guide-lines which stress the importance of joint activities and cooperation with peers As an aside it is worth commenting on the fact that students in higher education are sometimes given 'mixed messages' on the value of discussion groups and problem solving groups. They are exhorted to cooperate in such groups but at the same time the assessment system may continue to reward only individual efforts.

Social benefits of tutorial groups

The comments from students that have been presented so far have focused largely on aspects of group processes or the more 'cognitive' benefits of tutorials. The interviews also explored whether or not the informants felt that tutorials had any wider 'social benefits', particularly in the first year of study. Opinion on this matter was divided. Although many students didn't identify their initial tutorials as having any particularly strong social benefits, others took a contrary position, as can be seen from the following two quotes. The first is from a woman who is a second year Sociology student:

S7 *"-- in first year it helps a lot: because if you're not in halls then you don't really know people on your course, these tutorials, you can make friends in your tutorials which helps you, doesn't make you feel so lonely --."* The second quote is from a second year male Social

History student: S8 *"-- in lectures, well first year there's about a hundred people in lectures and you don't meet any people but tutorials I think do help in that respect. Especially in first year when no one knows anyone. Yeah. I mean most of my friends now were in tutorials last year."*

On a related theme some students mentioned that it was quite a contrast moving from a school where they were well known to staff to an institution where they felt in the words of one that "there was no sort of community". They mentioned the value of contact with a member of staff leading a tutorial, and with peers in the group. At a time when there has been a large increase in student numbers in UK universities and when there is something of a move towards more 'independent' learning, there is a clear danger that some individuals will feel isolated, or even alienated, from the general life of the university. Tutorial or problem-solving groups may play a modest part in assisting some students to become more socially integrated within a totally new environment.

Exploring personal problems in understanding a topic in a tutorial

Aside from their main task, tutorials and problem-based learning groups led by lecturers can also serve the function of allowing students the opportunity to raise problems that they are having with some aspect of their course content. Students were asked in the present study if they felt that there had been enough opportunity in tutorials to explore particular problems with course subject matter, or not. Forty seven of the students provided responses which could be categorized. Sixteen felt that there had been sufficient opportunity given to explore particular problems they might have in understanding a topic, whereas seventeen felt that they had not received sufficient opportunity. Nine felt that this had varied. Five students did not reply directly to the question on whether had been sufficient opportunity to explore particular problems, but simply stated that they had never done so in a tutorial. Although a considerable number of students may have felt that there was not enough of a chance to explore particular problems in tutorials, students in general commented that most tutors could be approached privately about a problem outside of the tutorial hour.

A related question on whether students felt that in a tutorial they needed to be guarded or not in saying that they didn't understand something revealed that many did feel reluctant in a group setting to admit that they were experiencing a difficulty in comprehending some point or topic. The consequences that this lack of willingness to expose problems in understanding can often have in tutorials is captured sharply in the following quote from a male second year student: S9 *"I mean most of them [i.e. tutors] usually sort of ask if there's any problems and most people usually react with a blank look so they just carry on with things."*

Unwillingness to lose face with their peers was openly admitted by some students as being the reason for not raising problems that they were experiencing, as in this extract from a third year male student: S10 *"I think it's probably just human nature like that you don't want to be made a fool of in front of your mates."* Another student remarked on how all of the students in a group may be guarded in raising a problem because of the false belief that they are the only one who may be experiencing a difficulty with this topic - a belief which ties them up in a communication knot. S11 *"I think, like to think oh well, he must know it, he's not asking so he must know it and it goes all the way round that. [slight laugh]"*

More altruistic reasons for being guarded about raising difficulties were expressed in quite a number of interviews, as the following quote from a second year female student studying Social History and Politics reveals: S12 *"I don't see there's anything wrong if people do perhaps want to bring up something they don't understand in a tutorial, but I sort of think oh hec I don't want to waste other people's time."* A similar view is evident in the following

90

extracts from a first year male Social History student who also had the conception that the exploration of personal problems in understanding is "more a private thing". S13 *"I think that's more a private thing actually, you know, if people do have problems they go and see their tutor but [in the tutorial] it's sort of like holding up discussion -- if you have a problem like that then I think it's better to see someone privately, so you can get it sorted out yourself. You can have your own conversation as long as it takes, and you're not holding up other people. I think that, you know, I'd feel selfish if I did that in a tutorial."*

On the question of raising difficulties with a tutor, one student drew attention to how difficult an exercise this may be for someone who is a complete novice in a subject. An articulate, academically able second year student, by her own volition rather than in response to any question of mine, commented on the problems that students may have in the early stages of their university career in resolving difficulties in understanding course content. A lack of subject knowledge, of an understanding of the exact standards that will be used to judge their academic work, or of familiarity with the forms of academic discourse could all singly or in combination be responsible for the state of affairs which she describes in the following extract. S14 *"It's all very well saying to people sort of ask whatever questions you want but very often when you come to university, you don't know what questions you want to ask. So there'll be some embarrassed silence and somebody 'd ask when the next exams were. But that wasn't the information that we really needed to know."*

Discussing this comment with her it was established that she was very much pointing to the need at that early stage of a university career to have help from a tutor in shaping a problem, but that such actions would not be necessary in subsequent years. Put in a slightly different way, she was drawing attention to the distinction between knowing that you are in a difficulty and having a more clearly formulated problem that someone has helped you to construct. One would expect students as they progress in their academic career to be able to take on fully responsibility for communicating their difficulties to members of staff: but the concern raised in the above extract indicates the need for tutors to be more pro-active in assisting students who are novices in a discipline.

Actively debating a point with another student
Moving on to another aspect of tutorials and problem-based learning groups, an important aim of higher education is to enable students to acquire the skill of cogently debating a point in a socially appropriate manner. Accordingly it seemed necessary in the interviews with students to explore how they felt in a tutorial about debating a point with their peers. (I was very careful in wording questions to students about this matter, and in my manner of speech, to make clear that I was enquiring about how happy they felt about engaging in debate on an academic matter, as distinct from a personal challenge of any sort; and that there was no implication that challenging a peer on a point needed to be performed in a confrontational style).

Forty-six of the student interviews provided data on this matter. Twenty of the forty-six stated that they were quite happy to debate a point with a fellow student, and seven were fairly happy but with certain reservations. One fourth year student, (who from my observations I knew to be very talkative in tutorials), said that he had never done so, and a third year woman student said that this was "not for me". Another student in his third year said that he wouldn't directly but would try to raise the point through the tutor. Three expressed very large reservations and indicated this was something they would seldom, if ever, do. Thirteen expressed either some or strong reservations.

The reasons given for not wishing to engage other students in debate varied considerably from student to student, but lack of sufficient subject knowledge per se about the topic of debate was a common reason. Another theme which emerged in a number of comments was not so much lack of subject knowledge, but a reluctance to engage in debate unless one felt very "sure" about the strength of one's argument or knowledge of a topic. The fear of losing face, to some degree or other appeared in some interviews. Conversely, a number of the students stated that their willingness to challenge other students on a point was very much inhibited by social sensitivity, a concern as to how any challenge would be perceived from the other person's perspective. A facilitative attitude on the part of the tutor and an informal, safe social atmosphere in the tutorial group were matters which were highlighted in some accounts as increasing willingness to debate.

The following three short extracts give a flavour of the factors which students identified as constraining their willingness to debate points. The first statement from a first year psychology student describes straightforward differences in terms of background knowledge in the subjects he mentions and points up the fact that willingness to engage in debate may vary considerably across subjects. S15 *"Eh, in Psychology, yes. I mean Philosophy of Science, I'm not really well read in that so I wouldn't in that. No."*

The second extract from a first year Nursing Studies student who is also studying Psychology as an outside subject starts off in much the same vein, but then she expands on how she might decide not to debate within a Psychology tutorial. S16 *"It depends how well I knew the subject. And also again if like in Psychology because I'm not still very sure about the subject, if I had a feeling maybe I don't really agree with that. If I could just make the comment I don't really agree with that, because and then they could come back. But if it was like I said if it was expanded, they said well why do you think that; why, what are you basing that on I, I wouldn't feel so confident in maybe being able to answer that. And so I tend not to. Unless I, unless I felt very strongly - I'd probably. Then I also I'd probably sit there thinking about it too long and then the conversation would pass over - then I'd lose space for it."*

In the third extract a second year Sociology student mentions the need to be sensitive to other people's feelings and presents a conception of himself as not having a sufficiently "qualified", authoritative voice in any debate. It is worth mentioning that this was a student who was quite able. He made clear that he did prepare for tutorials; and I have evidence from my own observations that he had prepared well for a short paper which he gave in one tutorial. S17 *"I think it's, it's down to how - thinking how they'd feel if someone did that to me, or thinking how I'd feel if someone did that to me."* Interviewer *"Do you want to say then how you feel, if you do say something to someone and a student challenges it?"* S17 *"Ah. [laughs] I don't suppose I'd mind actually. I don't know it - it. I think it's got a lot to do with the sort of qualification of the question. If it's a qualified - if you feel it's qualified or not: and I think I'd quite often feel it difficult to, to ask someone a qualified question when I'm just sort of in the same position as them."*

Drawing out some of the implications for practice in conducting small groups of the comments which I received from students, it is clearly reasonable to expect students to come to groups well enough prepared to be able to engage their peers in debate. For the tutor's part he or she can help to create the 'safe', supportive social atmosphere which would seem from the students' comments to be an important influence on their willingness to debate. It also needs to be recognized that arguing vigorously and clearly but in an 'impersonal'' fashion is a skill and a form of talk that may need to be consciously cultivated by various means rather than expected to emerge spontaneously over the course of a students undergraduate career.

Preferences for how debate is structured

Another topic which it seemed important to explore was how students reacted to tutorials which were structured in contrasting ways. Tutors can vary considerably in the way they conduct tutorials, some preferring a style which keeps discussion clearly and fairly tightly focused on a topic, or set of topics, while others prefer to have a rather more wide-ranging discussion. When the students in the sample were questioned on whether they preferred a more focused or more free-ranging discussion an interesting pattern of findings emerged. There is data on this topic for fifty-one of the fifty two interviews. Eighteen students preferred a fairly wide ranging to wide ranging discussion, and sixteen students preferred a fairly focused to focused discussion. Nine elected for a 'middle of-the-road' position. Seven students didn't state an overall preference but said, in the words of one, "that depends on the subject". One student was of the opinion that discussion should be clearly focused in the first two years of a students degree and more free-ranging in the third and fourth years.

The following two quotes give some sense of how students commented on this matter. The quotes come from two women students who were members of the same third year Economic and Social History tutorial group.

S18 *"I want it to be always very focused. I want it. I don't like them to be just. They are a waste of time if you just sit there and everyone just talks about what they feel like talking about."* S5 *"I don't like that when tutors focus all the time because I think that's wrong --- it is to me very important to understand the relationship between two things which maybe initially you don't think of relating but as you go to discussion you think oh maybe they are, and I think that that's very important."*

Some of the descriptions given by students of their preference for either a more focused or wide-ranging discussion can be seen to have parallels with the contrast which Pask (1976) has drawn between *serialist* and *holist* learning styles. The serialist learner prefers a fairly narrow focus on the material that is to be mastered, building up understanding in a step-by-step logical manner. By contrast, the holist sets out to learn new material by attempting to gain a broad overview of the topic and delights in illustrations and analogies. In reviewing the implications of Pask's work for teaching and learning in higher education, Entwistle (1992, p.21) remarks on how: "If lecturers exhibit extreme lecturing styles, either holist or serialist, it seems inevitable that students with the opposite style will find those classes uncongenial and difficult. Yet lecturers are free to indulge their own stylistic preferences, however extreme, while students have to make the best of relative degrees of mismatch with their own preferences." The descriptions given by students of their preferences for a focused or wide-ranging discussion would seem to indicate that a very similar set of comments apply to tutorial groups, as well as lecturing.

Clearly a direct matching of the learning/teaching style of a tutor and of the students in his or her group is not a feasible exercise. However, tutors need to be alert to the effects that the adoption of an extreme style of structuring discussion may have on some of the students in their group. It is also to be hoped that over the course of their undergraduate career students will be exposed to an appropriate range of different styles of lecturing, tutorials, problem-based work and coursework demands. This variety of experience may encourage them to adopt the *versatile* style of learning, using both global and analytical processes where appropriate, that Pask suggest is best suited for achieving a high quality of understanding.

Differing conceptions and purposes

Turning from the question of preferences for contrasting styles of tutorials, I want to conclude the presentation of findings by looking at the differences that existed between students in their accounts of their own purposes in tutorials. Many of the students whom I interviewed made sharply critical comments about how some of the individual tutorial groups they had experienced throughout their university career had been conducted. However, with only a few exceptions they saw tutorials as a useful form of organizing learning in higher education. There were differences between individuals in how they conceived of the usefulness of tutorials. Extracts from three of the student interviews are presented here to give some sense of how their purposes varied. Some students had a few different goals which might also vary according to context, but for the purposes of clear exposition in this brief chapter three interviews have been chosen where there was one very dominant theme. The first set of extracts comes from an interview with a fourth year Psychology student who enjoys debate as an end in itself and is intent on negotiating with others a new understanding of a topic. To add some context to the reading of these quotes, at one point in the interview he drew a contrast between school and university, seeing fewer barriers and greater equality between teachers and learners in higher education. From my own observations of Psychology tutorials in which he took part, he does indeed debate in the style indicated in his statements.

Active Debater

S4 " -- obviously it's important to get - I mean a lot of different people, different views to be discussing. And that's, I mean that's really what I'd like our tutorials [to be] - to get different people with differing views discussing things." "-- somewhere where you could question ideas more and I mean debate more." "I suppose that one of the values of a university is I mean becoming aware that there is more than one interpretation that can be given to research: and discussion by its nature, implies by its nature that there has to be a couple of valid viewpoints to be discussed, otherwise there isn't any discussion."

The second extract gives a sense of the conception that a fourth year Nursing studies student, (for whom English was a second language), had of the purposes of tutorials. At various points in the interview she stressed that their purpose should be the clarification of ideas and personal understanding and that this was what she hoped to achieve from tutorials.

Gaining greater clarity of understanding

S19 "-- the aim of the tutorial is to clarify something. If you don't clarify these things you just speak and, you know, like if you have a nice discussion around a cup of coffee and you know, say your value system. The tutorial is different. It's to try to, to clarify, to declaim your knowledge of something that has been introduced to you during a lecture ---. But it's not just discussion idea - there is certain concepts that need clarification. And also it should be the tutorial, a place where there should be room for that, [to] come out that well, OK, I don't understand that." Elsewhere in the interview she noted her dissatisfaction with tutorials where there was "woffly discussion" and the aim of clarification was not achieved. The third extract from a second year student studying Social History and Politics is straightforward and speaks for itself.

Practice in Communication Skills

S20 " Coming here this morning, I thought right what am I going to say - I think the main thing I have to say about tutorials is I don't learn a great deal practically from them, as I didn't learn the subject - it's regurgitated lectures most of the time and I'm not saying that should be changed because I think it's very good - the opportunity for us to communicate with other people. Ehm. I suppose communication and presentation of yourself and your opinions is, is for me the main aspect of a tutorial. And that is what I get out of it - it makes me think

I can stand up for myself and can say what I like in front of people who I know may not necessarily agree."

Given that there is some variety in the manner in which students appear to conceive of the usefulness of tutorials, it would seem to be important that tutors leading discussions or problem-solving groups themselves present very clearly their own aims and their expectations concerning student purposes. These differences between students in how they construct their purposes in tutorials and other differences which have been noted earlier in the chapter also bring into focus a simple but major methodological point concerning the study of talk and problem solving in natural settings. It is important that attention is not focused too narrowly on the form of academic discourse, dialogic processes and problem-solving processes. In looking at what is achieved in, and by, talk in higher education settings it is also necessary to consider how the quality and nature of discussion is shaped to a certain extent by the knowledge base, learning styles and purposes of the individual student participants (Anderson, 1991).

References

Anderson, C. (1991) Negotiating Understanding. Paper presented at the 4th EARLI conference, Turku, Finland, August 1991.

Brown, G. and Atkins, M. (1988) **Effective Teaching in Higher Education.** London: Methuen.

Cawley, P. (1991) A Problem-based Module in Mechanical Engineering. In: D. Boud & G. Feletti. (eds) **The Challenge of Problem Based Learning.** London: Kogan Page.

Entwistle, N. (1992) **The Impact of Teaching on Learning Outcomes in Higher Education: A Literature Review.** Sheffield: Universities' Staff Development Unit.

Jaques, D. (1992) **Learning in Groups.** 2nd. edn. London: Kogan Page.

Pask, G. 1976. Learning Styles and Strategies. **British Journal of Educational Psychology,** 46, 4-11.

chapter 11

Combining system-based and problem-based approaches in medical education

Th. Olle ten Cate & Egbert Schadé

Introduction

Introducing problem-based learning is often regarded as an all-or-nothing choice. A curriculum with some traditional elements together with problem-based elements may generate tensions if these elements together are not part of a well structured complete curriculum. Slowly introducing PBL step by step, leaving other parts of the curriculum in their conventional state may be confusing for students as to the demands the curriculum asks from them. A complete reform at once has many advantages. This, however, does not exclude the benefits of a deliberate reform into a curriculum in which both a system-based and a problem-based approach has its place.

In this chapter the advantages of combining elements of problem-based learning with a more traditional system-based approach in higher education is explored. Specifically, in education with both scientific and vocational[1] characteristics, both approaches are valuable in reaching the educational goals. The example comprises the training in medicine, a field in which much educational development and research has been done. However, the reader may well translate the arguments to other scientific-vocational studies.

Before going into the specifics of medical training, it is necessary to give a definition of the systematic (i.e. system-based) and field-driven information processing and retrieval in education, which will be referred to below. The system-based information processing and retrieval is based on educational goals, set by the teaching institution, and is characterized by a logical, coherent and chronological presentation of content materials. To foster a growth of knowledge in students, regular examinations are held. Field-driven information processing and retrieval on the other hand is dictated by events in a vocational environment. Here, chance of encounter influences what is learned and can be retrieved. Furthermore, there is no control over the attainment of detailed educational goals.

In system-based information processing the point of reference is a coherent description of a system (e.g., an organ system or a health care system in medicine, a Newtonian Law in physics, a theory in psychology etc.). In field-driven (problem-based) information processing the point of reference is formed by observed phenomena. Here specific information is to be converted or constructed to a system-description. In a sense, both methods of information processing have opposite directions. A system-based approach does not necessarily imply a discipline-oriented approach, just as a problem-based

---

1) in this text the term 'vocational' indicates general training for a profession and not specifically postgraduate training for a medical specialism

approach does not necessarily exclude a discipline-oriented approach.

There may be little difference in the knowledge base resulting from an systematic and a field-driven information processing. However, the possibilities to use this knowledge may be very different. Specifically in education with a vocational character systematic education may often be advocated: certification should guarantee the necessary knowledge and skills to perform the intended job. On the other hand, the student should master a field-driven retrieval potential of the knowledge and skills. This tension will be illustrated below. Figure 1 shows a schematic representation of this distinction.

Figure 1: Systematic and field driven information processing and retrieval

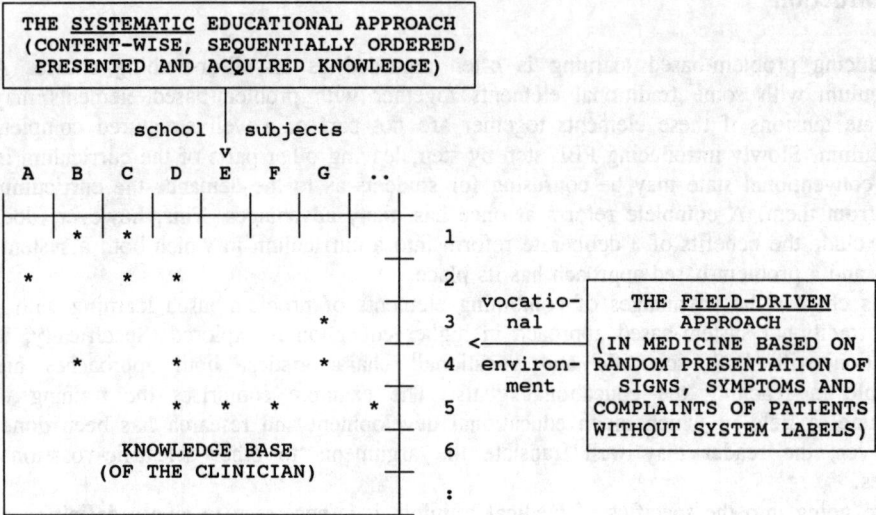

```
┌─────────────────────────────────────────────┐
│ THE SYSTEMATIC EDUCATIONAL APPROACH          │
│ (CONTENT-WISE, SEQUENTIALLY ORDERED,         │
│  PRESENTED AND ACQUIRED KNOWLEDGE)           │
└─────────────────────────────────────────────┘

          school │ subjects
                 v
  A   B   C   D   E   F   G   ..
┌──┬──┬──┬──┬──┬──┬──┬──┬──┐
│  │ *│ *│  │  │  │  │  │  │  1
│ *│  │ *│ *│  │  │  │  │  │  2                 ┌──────────────────────────┐
│  │  │  │  │  │ *│  │  │  │  3    vocatio-     │   THE FIELD-DRIVEN        │
│  │  │  │  │  │  │  │  │  │        nal         │      APPROACH             │
│ *│  │ *│  │  │ *│  │  │  │  4  <──            │ (IN MEDICINE BASED ON     │
│  │  │ *│ *│ *│  │ *│  │  │  5    environ-     │ RANDOM PRESENTATION OF    │
│  │  │  │  │  │  │  │  │  │        ment        │ SIGNS, SYMPTOMS AND       │
│      KNOWLEDGE BASE          │  6            │ COMPLAINTS OF PATIENTS    │
│     (OF THE CLINICIAN)       │  :            │ WITHOUT SYSTEM LABELS)    │
└──────────────────────────────┘               └──────────────────────────┘
```

Retrieval of knowledge-elements to solve a vocational problem may call on scattered parts of systematically acquired knowledge

Medical education

The primary objective of the training of medical students may be formulated as the competence of solving medical problems, i.e. diagnostic, therapeutical or general health-care problems. The practice of medicine can essentially be viewed as a cognitive problem-solving activity (Patel & Patel, 1990). Yet, students seem to have difficulty in handling patient problems when they enter the clinical ward, even after years of medical education (Barrows, 1984; Boshuizen & Essed, 1990). Moss & McManus (1992) found that the risk of getting diagnoses wrong is a major source of anxiety of most students beginning their clinical training. The issue is therefore: how can they be better prepared for clinical problem solving? Designing adequate instructional procedures that lead toward this objective requires both knowledge of clinical problem solving and knowledge of effective instructional methods.

Essentials of clinical problem solving

The competence of solving clinical problems, most comprehensively summarized as a cyclical reasoning process of generating hypotheses, inquiry and testing hypotheses (Barrows et al. 1982), appears to be highly content-specific. Research on clinical problem solving indicates that there does not seem to be a content-free clinical problem-solving skill one can simply acquire (Norman, 1984). Being able to solve problem A does not imply the ability to solve problem B, even in the same content-domain (Norman et al., 1985; Ronteltap & Imbos, 1990; Weverling et al., 1992). In other words, there appears to be limited transfer of this skill from one problem to another. The ability to solve clinical problems may to a large extent depend on experience in patient care (Elstein et al, 1978). Experience with specific patients and their clinical context seems to facilitate the retention of clinical information (Hobus et al., 1987), even if irrelevant information is presented (Van Rossum et al., 1990; Van Rossum et al., 1991). It appears that experienced physicians possess a skill (have a 'clinical view') that they are often not able to explain to others and that therefore seems somewhat magical (Ridderikhof, 1991). Research indicates that basic (biomedical) knowledge is used in a - experientially learned -shortened manner during cognitive diagnostic procedures (Boshuizen, 1989), especially in 'predictive reasoning' (i.e. hypothesis-based). Earlier confrontations with similar medical problems substantially contribute to the ease of solving a particular medical problem, especially in 'data-driven reasoning' (i.e. non-hypothesis based - Patel, Evans & Kaufman, 1990). A broad skill in clinical problem solving probably therefore may require both the systematic building of a detailed causal knowledge base and a broad clinical experience (Schmidt & Boshuizen, in press).

Medical schools are faced with the task of designing instructional procedures in such a way that the above skill will - eventually - be mastered by the future physician. Indeed a significant problem, since clearly practicing as a doctor seems necessary to acquire that skill (Ridderikhof, 1991). Although little time is available to reach this goal, extensive clinical experience should somehow be realized in the curriculum.

The development of expertise in clinical problem solving

Generally a distinction is made between basic-science ('biomedical') knowledge and clinical knowledge, both assumed to be necessary in solving clinical problems. Usually biomedical knowledge is acquired first and clinical knowledge afterward. A consistent finding is that students starting the clinical period of education do not adequately use biomedical knowledge in problem solving (Balla et al., 1990) even if they do possess this knowledge (Patel et al., 1988), a well-known complaint of clinical teachers. Apparently some process is needed to let students use their biomedical knowledge when clinically needed.

Boshuizen (1989) postulates a process in which (i) basic-science knowledge is acquired, (ii) 'compilation' of this knowledge occurs to shorter and more flexible knowledge, (iii) information of patients enriches this knowledge and finally (iv) mental 'disease scripts' develop. These scripts operate as mental frames of reference to evaluate new clinical problems. Clinical knowledge may, however, be viewed as a knowledge base, separately established from the biomedical knowledge base. In 1990 Boshuizen & Schmidt suggest the existence of a three-stage model: "In the first stage biomedical and clinical knowledge develop separately with an emphasis on biomedical knowledge. In the second stage, taking place in the clerkship period during which students are for the first time exposed to real-life clinical cases, emphasis is shifted towards the acquisition of clinical knowledge. The final stage is reached when both knowledge bases have matured to a sufficient extent, and compilation of biomedical knowledge and integration into clinical knowledge occurs". More recent work suggests further that in solving medical problems clinicians first search their mind for prior examples from earlier experience, and when these are not available they resort to causal biomedical knowledge (Schmidt & Boshuizen, in press). The foundation of domain-specific (i.e. biomedical) knowledge as a prerequisite to efficient and effective utilization of strategic knowledge has been stated by others (Alexander & Judy, 1988). A second task for the medical school therefore arises: designing a curriculum in which efficient integration of biomedical knowledge within clinical knowledge is realized.

The search for instructional procedures leading to transfer

The quest for instructional procedures that lead to broad, stable problem solving skills, with as wide transfer as possible, is of course not characteristic for medical education alone. Lack of transfer outside the content-domain ('far transfer') is often found with the teaching of cognitive skills; transfer within the content-domain ('near transfer') may or may not occur (De Corte, 1987; Simons & Verschaffel, 1992). McKeachie (1987) points out that the word 'transfer' usually implies close resemblance between the original situation and the new situation. When the distance is larger one speaks of 'problem solving' and application of a cognitive skill in a very different situation may be called 'creativity'. How should the intermediate-distance transfer of 'problem solving' be best trained?

Salomon and Globerson (1987) use the distinction between a 'low road' (automatic) transfer and a 'high road' transfer, i.e. resulting from a deliberate mindful abstraction from non-essential features of a presented example. Assuming that both types of transfer are useful objectives of (medical) education, 'low road'-transfer requires practice and 'high road'-transfer requires mindful abstraction, for instance through verbalization of meaningful understanding, analogical reasoning etcetera. Being mindful or not may be viewed as a personality characteristic of students (Salomon and Globerson, 1987). McKeachie, however, suggests trying to induce a *habit* of mindfulness through giving attention to it in subsequent courses and to foster mindful transfer through methods that realize achievement motivation. Sufficient self-competence and achievement motivation he considers necessary for mindful transfer: 'unmotivated learners are likely to withdraw or proceed mindlessly' (McKeachie, 1987). Vermunt (1989) advocates a process-oriented instruction as a means to stimulate self-regulation of learning, after stages of teacher-controlled learning and a 'shared control' of the learning process, i.e. under control of the teacher and the student together. This approach may well turn out to stimulate the internal motivation, necessary for high road transfer that occurs in problem solving.

This short overview suggests applying educational procedures in the medical curriculum that stress mindful abstraction through cognitive tasks (e.g.., verbalization, analogical reasoning - fostering high road transfer), frequent practice (for low road transfer) and an educational setting that stimulates self-regulation of learning.

Current approaches in medical education

Since decades medical educators have shown concern for the lack of the problem solving skills of students in their clinical clerkships (Gerritsma & Smal, 1973). Most of the recent transitions several medical curricula show (Harden et al., 1984) in curriculum structure, content, instructional methods and testing methods (at least thirteen separate trends can be distinguished in Dutch curricula - Ten Cate, 1988) are somehow linked to the wish to teach problem solving skills. Integration of basic science and clinical subjects into theme-wise entities, clinical demonstrations early in the curriculum, small-group education, training of clinical skills before entering clinical wards and the introduction of simulated patient techniques all hope to prepare students better for dealing with patient problems. Notably one approach has internationally served as a model: the Problem Based Learning (PBL) curriculum, designed by Barrows et al.. (Barrows and Tamblyn, 1980). Basically in this curriculum students are, from the very beginning, continuously confronted with problems, serving as the major stimuli to acquire knowledge: basic science, biomedical, social and clinical problems. It is expected that students from these curricula will be better prepared for patient care, i.e. for solving (clinical) problems. Do these curricular changes help?

Since some years comparative studies of PBL versus conventional[2] curricula appear in the literature (Bender et al., 1984; Coles, 1985; Newble & Clark, 1986; Schmidt et al., 1987; Santos-Gomez et al., 1990; Friedman et al., 1990; Van Hessen et al., 1991; Patel et al., 1991; Moore, 1991; Norman & Schmidt, 1992). It appears that, as far as factual knowledge (especially in the basic sciences) is concerned, alumni from non-PBL schools seem to score at the same or somewhat better level than alumni from PBL schools, although their advantage may disappear over time (Norman & Schmidt, 1992). When problem solving skills are compared, the results are still inconclusive. Santos-Gomez et al. (1990) find no difference in critical thinking and independent learning between PBL and non-PBL educated residents, as judged by clinical supervisors and nurses. Patel et al.. finds that PBL-students show the type of systematic thinking that has been taught: more backward reasoning, more systematic use of clinical information, more elaboration and generation of multiple diagnostic explanations through hypothetico-deductive reasoning. However, the PBL students also tend to make more errors in their explanations than non-PBL students (Patel et al., 1991).

There has undoubtedly been made much progress in techniques of instructing problem solving skills by the concept of problem-based learning. In some respects, however, PBL may possibly be less effective. Patel et al. (1991), as well as Boshuizen & Schmidt (1990), point out a potential danger of full integration of clinical and biomedical education. "If the two domains are so different and independent of each other, it makes considerable sense to teach them in distinct units. Moreover, a considerable amount of confusion may be avoided by ensuring that one of the two domains (biomedical or clinical) is highly overlearned before the other is encountered. In fact, the use of erroneous basic science explanations by the PBL-curriculum students, even in the context

---

2) We believe the term 'conventional' or 'traditional' curricula, as non-PBL curricula are often called, implies an underestimation of the great variance among them and a disregard of the innovations they have often gone through. However, since this terminology is widely used, we will abide by it.

of correct clinical diagnoses, indicates that there is a genuine danger of such confusion in an integrated curriculum" (Patel et al., 1991). Indeed, problem-based learning is primarily designed as a general didactic method and not a specific instructional tool to learn *clinical* problem solving; the method is applied in many different curricula. Learning to solve problems is *not* the central objective in PBL (Wijnen & Schmidt, 1986). Expecting better solving of clinical problems in PBL-alumni should therefore not be justified only because of their PBL-curriculum, since, as we have seen, problem solving skills are highly content-specific. Among the outcome measures in PBL versus conventional curricula clinical problem solving skills are considered *not* differ (Friedman et al, 1990).

Preparation for clinical problem solving at the University of Amsterdam

Recapitulating the above mentioned requirements for training of problem solving skills the following suggestions can be distinguished:
1 confront students with *many*, *different* and *relevant* clinical problems and this way build 'clinical' experience
2 integrate biomedical and clinical teaching in such a way that the domains facilitate and not hinder each other; domain-specific biomedical knowledge should form a basis.
3 formulate cognitive tasks to foster mindful abstraction
4 realize frequent practice and rehearsal
5 stimulate self-regulation of learning
In designing the latest medical curriculum at the University of Amsterdam[3] these requirements have been tried to be met. The framework of the preclinical curriculum consists of a combination of (a) integrated blocks (80%) and (b) line-wise clinical teaching (20%)[4].
(a) The blocks all have a theme-wise, objective-based, multidisciplinary content, in which basic *and* clinical sciences are combined. Central issues in these blocks are 'patho-biological' concepts with clinical relevance. Basic-science subjects are taught from the point of view of relevance for patho-biology. Clinical topics, i.e. diseases with their characteristics, are related to the patho-biological concepts and are systematically taught within the blocks. All blocks close with a formal examination of biomedical and (systematic) clinical knowledge.
(b) The line-wise clinical teaching is designed to train clinical problem solving. Every week one day (more in the higher years) is devoted to (i) clinical demonstrations and modelling of the problem solving by clinical teachers (ii) practicing of cognitive skills in clinical problem solving in small groups and (iii) training of psychomotor and verbal skills. These three are increasingly integrated during the years. The point of departure in (i) and (ii) is not the systematic approach (cf. the blocks) but, invariably, some clinical manifestation of a patient-case. In dealing with this case, knowledge of prior block-themes is required. The line-wise clinical education in this way constantly applies prior systematically taught biomedical and clinical knowledge in clinical situations. Very little

---

3) This curriculum development has been a cooperative effort with the medical Faculty of the Free University of Amsterdam

4) apart from individual practicals (e.g. nurse-aid period, research period)

new content-information is presented, only when necessary to understand a specific case. Figure 2 shows an overview of this curriculum.

Figure 2: Outline of the preclinical curriculum

Block 1	Block 2	Block 3	Block 4	Block 5	Block 6
Ill and healthy people	From molecule to cell	From cell to tissue	On human, physician & Society	Organ systems	Nurse aid practical
Clinical line education					

Block 7	Block 8	Block 9	Block 10	Block 11	Block 12	Junior clerckships Research week Block Help and Care
Bio-regu-lations	Blood, oncology & genes	Infection & resistance	Heart & circulation	Respiratory functions	Kidney's & interior environm.	
Clinical line education						

(cont.) Junior clerkships Research week Block Help and Care	Block 13	Block 14	Block 15	Block 16	Block Science	Re-search term and elec-tives
	Nervous system	Psychic functioning	Nutrition & digestion	Procreation		
	Clinical line education					

(cont.) Research term and electives	Block 17	Block 18 Stages of life & sexuality	Block 19	Block 20
	Movement		Sensory organs & skin	Health care
	Clinical line education			

Specifically the small group training (ii), also called the 'Workshops Clinical Decision-making' is designed to meet the educational requirements of active practice, building experience, exerting cognitive tasks and stimulation of self-regulation of learning. To this end a peer teaching format has been chosen. Groups of twelve students meet every three weeks during year 2 through 4. Each session one to three clinical cases are in discussion. Cases consist of a written introduction of the patient with his or her clinical manifestations and a series of questions (e.g., what would your hypothesis be? what patho-biological bases do you have for this opinion? what epidemiological reasons do you have to expect outcome X? etc.). Of each group three students operate as 'referents' and are provided subsidiary information on the case (such as results of laboratory tests). Referents are considered relative experts and to lead the session, including the discussion. They may be asked to give a mini-lecture during the case presentation on a prior assigned relevant topic, to help proceed the problem solving process. Each group has a permanent clinical teacher to guide the learning process and to assess the performance of the referents and - marginally - the other students. Active participation is required and each student has a referent function once every four sessions. All students are expected to read some assigned material and prepare answers to the questions. Furthermore, the cases are designed to incorporate knowledge of prior blocks making it necessary for students to keep up with their studies and to regularly review material. Specifically the referent function may stimulate active elaboration of prior knowledge (Ten Cate, 1986), which is considered beneficial for retention (Schmidt, 1982) and clinical thinking (Coles, 1990).

Summarizing the PBL-elements that have been incorporated

Characteristics of problem-based learning that have been incorporated in this curriculum are notably (a) the small-group format with (b) the non-directive function of the tutor (here called the 'consultant') and (c) the active part students play in this small-group education. To test students' clinical-line knowledge (d) a clinical progress-test has been added to the block tests that are regularly held. This test is to cover the clinically-relevant knowledge of the curriculum and is administered every semester in the second, third and fourth year. The test, developed together with the Medical Faculty of the Free University of Amsterdam is yet in a developmental stage (Sagasser et al., 1992).

Clearly there remain many differences with a complete PBL-curriculum. The major distinction however is not the extent of the problem-based elements in the curriculum. It is the different goal of the Workshops Clinical Decision-making. The workshops do not aim at acquiring new knowledge, but applying already, systematically, gained knowledge. In PBL, learning to solve problems is not the paramount objective, in the Workshops it is.

This curriculum has started in 1990/1991. Too little time has passed yet to present substantial evaluation data. Our first impressions (from simple evaluation forms) are that students as well as clinical teachers appreciate this teaching method and that the training of clinical problem solving may be effectively realized within this format.

References

Alexander, P.A., & Judy, J.E. (1988) The interaction of domain-specific and strategic knowledge in academic performance **Review of educational research, 58**, 4, 375-404.

Balla, J.I., Biggs, J.B., Gibson, M., & Chang, A., (1990) The application of basic science concepts to clinical problem-solving **Medical Education, 24**, 2, 137-146.

Barrows, H.S. (1984) A specific problem-based, self-directed learning method designed to teach medical problem-solving skills, and enhance knowledge retention and recall In H.G. Schmidt & M.L. de Volder (Eds.) **Tutorials in problem-based learning** (pp 16-32) Assen (the Netherlands): Van Gorcum & Comp. B.V.

Barrows, H.S., Norman, G.R., Neufield, V.R. & Feightner, J.W. (1982) The clinical reasoning of randomly selected physicians in general medical practice. **Clinical and Investigative Medicine, 5**, 49-55.

Barrows, H.S. & Tamblyn, R.M. (1980) **Problem-based learning, an approach to medical education** New York: Springer.

Bender, W., Cohen - Schotanus, J., Imbos, T., Versfeld, W.A., Verwijnen, M. (1984) Medische kennis bij studenten uit verschillende medische faculteiten: van hetzelfde laken een pak? **Nederlands tijdschrift voor geneeskunde, 128**, 917-921.

Boshuizen, H.P.A. (1989). **De ontwikkeling van medische expertise - een cognitief psychologische benadering**. Doctoral thesis, Haarlem/Amsterdam: Thesis.

Boshuizen, H.P.A. & Essed, G.G.M., (1990) Leren probleemoplossen in de stagefase; naar een didactiek voor het klinisch onderwijs In Slobbe, F.J., Blankestijn, J., Zeeuwen, O.S. C. & Willemsen, T.J.M. (Eds) **Terugblik op tien jaar studievaardigheden - toekomstige ontwikkelingen, Proceedings Landelijke Dag Studievaardigheden 1990**. Eindhoven: TUE/HE.

Boshuizen, H.P.A. & H.G. Schmidt, H.G. (1990) The role of biomedical knowledge in clinical reasoning by experts, intermediates and novices **Onderzoek van Onderwijs - report # 41**. Maastricht: Rijksuniversiteit Limburg.

Coles, C.R. (1985) Differences between conventional and problem-based curricula in their student's approaches to studying **Medical Education, 19**, 4, 308-309.

Coles, C.R. (1990) Elaborated learning in undergraduate medical education **Medical Education, 24**, 1, 14-22.

De Corte, E. (Ed.) (1987) Acquisition and transfer of knowledge and cognitive skills [Special issue] **International Journal of Educational Research, 11**, 6.

Elstein, A.S., Shulman, L.S. and Sprafka, S.A. (1978). **Medical Problem Solving: an analysis of clinical reasoning**, Cambridge, M.A.: Harvard University Press.

Friedman, C.P., De Bliek, R., Greer, D.S., Mennin, S.P., Norman, G.R., Sheps, C.G., Swanson, D.B., Woodward, C.A. (1990) Charting the winds of change: Evaluating innovative medical curricula, **Academic Medicine, 65**, 8-14.

Gerritsma, J.G.M. & Smal, J.A. (1974) **Grensverschuivingen in het medisch onderwijs** Utrecht: Oosthoek, Scheltema & Holkema.

Harden, R.M., Sowden, S. & Dunn, W.R., Educational strategies in curriculum development: the SPICES model. **Medical Education, 18**, 4, 284-297.

Hobus, P.P.M., Schmidt, H.G., Boshuizen , H.P.A. & Patel, V.L. (1987). Contextual factors in the activation of first diagnostic hypotheses: expert-novice differences. **Medical Education, 21**, 6, 471-476.

McKeachie, W.J. (1987) Cognitive skills and their transfer: discussion In De Corte, E. (Ed.) (1987) Acquisition and Transfer of Knowledge and Cognitive Skills **International Journal of Educational Research, 11**, 6.

Moore, G.T. (1991) The effect of compulsory participation of medical students in problem-based learning **Medical Education, 25**, 2, 140-143.

Moss, F. & McManus, I.C. (1992) The Anxieties of new clinical students, **Medical Education, 26**, 1, 17-20.

Newble, D.I. & Clarke, R.A. Comparison of the approaches to learning of students in a traditional and an innovative medical school Medical Education, 20, 162-175.

Norman, G.R. (1984) Clinical reasoning - introduction. In Schmidt, H.G. & De Volder, M. (Eds.) Tutorials in Problem-based Learning Vol.1, Assen/Maastricht: Van Gorcum.

Norman, G.R., Tugwell, P., Feightner, J.W., Muzzin, L.J., Jacoby, L.L. (1985). Knowledge and clinical problem solving. Medical Education, 19, 5, 344-356.

Norman, G.R. & Schmidt, H.G. (1992) The psychological basis of problem-based learning: a review of the evidence Academic Medicine, 67, 9, 557-565.

Patel, V.L., D.A. Evans & D.R. Kaufman (1990) Reasoning strategies and the use of biomedical knowledge by medical students, Medical Education, 24, 2, 129-136.

Patel, V.L., Groen. G.J. & Norman, G.R. (1991) Effects of conventional and problem-based medical curricula on problem solving Academic Medicine, 66, 7, 380-389.

Patel, V.L., Groen, G.J. & Scott, H.M. (1988) Biomedical knowledge in explanations of clinical problems by medical students. Medical Education, 22, 5, 398-406.

Patel, V.L. & Patel, Y.C. (1990). A cognitive framework for performance-based clinical competency. In W. Bender, R.J. Hiemstra, R.J., A.J.J.M. Scherpbier & R.P. Zwierstra (Eds.) Teaching and assessing clinical competence, Groningen: BoekWerk Publications.

Ridderikhof, J. (1991) Medical Problem-solving: an exploration of strategies Medical Education, 25, 196-207.

Ronteltap, C.F.M. & Imbos, T. (1990). The use of knowledge in diagnostic problem solving. In W. Bender, R.J. Hiemstra, A.J.J.M. Scherpbier & R.P. Zwierstra (Eds.) Teaching and assessing clinical competence, Groningen: BoekWerk Publications.
Sagasser, M.H., ten Cate, Th.J., Heijlman, J., (1992) Preliminary results of the assessment of clinical competence in the preclinical period In: Harden, R.M., Hart, I.R. & Mulholland, H. Approaches to the assessment of clinical competence, Dundee: Centre for Medical Education.

Salomon, G. & Globerson, T. (1987) Skill may not be enough: the role of mindfulness in learning and transfer In De Corte, E. (Ed.) (1987) Acquisition and Transfer of Knowledge and Cognitive Skills International Journal of Educational Research, 11, 6.

Santoz-Gomez, L., Kalishman, S., Rezler, B., Skipper, B. & Mennin, S.P. (1990) Residency performance of graduates from a problem-based and a conventional curriculum Medical Education, 24 , 4, 366-375.

Schmidt, H.G. (1982) Activatie van voorkennis, intrinsieke motivatie en de verwerking van tekst Doctoral dissertation, Apeldoorn: Van Walraven.

Schmidt, H.G., Dauphinee, W.D., Patel, V.L. (1987) Comparing the effects of problem-based and conventional curricula in an international sample Journal of Medical Education, 62, 4, 305-315.

Schmidt, H.G. & Boshuizen, H.P.A. (in press) On acquiring expertise in medicine **Educational Psychology Review.**

Simons, P.R.J. & Verschaffel, L. (1992) Transfer: onderzoek en onderwijs in P.R.J. Simons & L. Verschaffel (Eds.) Themanummer Transfer [Special issue] **Tijdschrift voor Onderwijsresearch, 17,** 1, 3-16.

Ten Cate, Th.J. (1986) **Leren in groepen zonder docent** Doctoral dissertation, Amsterdam: Bureau Faculteit Geneeskunde UvA.

Ten Cate, Th.J. (1988) Bakens voor nieuwe stappen in de ontwikkeling van de artsopleiding - **NPOG-memo 1988-IV** Amsterdam: Faculty of Medicine.

Van Hessen, P.A.W., Verwijnen, GT.M. & Imbos, Tj., De kennis van de Nederlandse basisarts, gemeten met de Maastrichtse voortgangstoets, **Nederlands Tijdschrift voor Geneeskunde, 135,** 42, 1975-1978.

Van Rossum, H.J.M., Bender, W., Meinders, A.E., (1991). De invloed van biografische details in casuistische mededelingen op het diagnostisch oordeel. **Nederlands Tijdschrift voor Geneeskunde, 135,** 18, 802-805.

Van Rossum, H.J.M., Briët, E., Bender, W. & Meinders, A.E. (1990). The transfer effect of one single patient demonstration on diagnostic judgement of undergraduate medical students: both for better and worse. In W. Bender, R.J. Hiemstra, R.J., A.J.J.M. Scherpbier & R.P. Zwierstra (Eds.) **Teaching and assessing clinical competence,** Groningen: BoekWerk Publications.

Vermunt, J.D.H.M. (1989) **The interplay between internal and external regulation of learning, and the design of process-oriented instruction** Paper presented at the third Conference of the European Association of Research on Learning and Instruction, Madrid, September 1989.

Weverling, G.J., Stam, J., ten Cate, Th.J. & van Crevel, H. (1992) **Computer based teaching of to improve clinical problem-solving by medical students: a randomized controlled trial** In: Harden, R.M., Hart, I.R. & Mulholland, H. **Approaches to the assessment of clinical competence,** Dundee: Centre for Medical Education.

Wijnen, W.H.F.W., & Schmidt, H.G. (1986) Probleemgestuurd onderwijs bij de medische faculteit in Maastricht. In Mettes, C.T.C.W., & Gerritsma, J.G.M. (Eds.) **Probleemoplossen** Aula 819 Utrecht: Het Spectrum BV.